The Power of Blended Learning in the Sciences

Dr. Oliver Dreon
Dr. Ivan A. Shibley, Jr.
Dr. Timothy D. Wilson

First Edition

To order, contact:

The Part-Time Press

P.O. Box 130117

Ann Arbor, MI 48113-0117

Phone/Fax: 734-930-6854

First printing: March, 2019

© 2019 The Part-Time Press

ISBN: 978-0-940017-46-7 (paperback)

Printed in the United States of America

Table of Contents

PREFACE: WHY BLEND SCIENCE INSTRUCTION?..........*10*
How To Get the Most Out of This Book 19

PART I REASONS TO BLEND 20

CHAPTER 1 NEUROBIOLOGY PRIMER: THE THINK ORGAN 21
The Thinking Organ 21
Neuronal Anatomy 22
Reducing Cognitive Load.. 24
Multimedia Learning... 26

CHAPTER 2 EFFECTIVELY TEACHING WHAT YOU KNOW 28
Where Do I Start? 28
Teaching Best Practices 29
Pedagogical Content Knowledge (PCK)....................... 31

CHAPTER 3 BLENDING—GIMME A "B..." 36
What's in a Name?.. 36
B-Balanced 38
L-Learner-Centered 39
E-Engagement-Driven.. 39
N-Novel.. 40
D-Data-Driven 41
Self-Study Questions for Blended Design 41

PART II THE BLENDED CYCLE..............................42

CHAPTER 4 BLENDING—WHEN STUDENTS LEARN WITHOUT YOU 43
Organization 44
Learning Outcomes 45
Pre-Class Assignments 46
Pre-Class Videos 46
Screencasting... 47
Student Responsibility.. 49
Preparing for F2F Time.. 51

CHAPTER 5 IN-CLASS LEARNING: KEEP IT ACTIVE......53
Learner-Centered Teaching..53
Time 56
Engaging Students/Active Learning 57
Technology in Class...58
Synchronizing Your Course 60
A Lesson on Evolution 61
A Physics Course..61

CHAPTER 6 LEARNING AFTER CLASS: INCORPORATING
FAILURE INTO YOUR LESSON PLAN...............63
Rehearsal 65
Self-Testing...66
Activities at Higher Levels of Cognition.........................67
Transparency 68

PART III TECHNOLOGY FOR BLENDING...............70

CHAPTER 7 THE TECH ADVANTAGE 71
Emma: Easily Distracted..72
Jamal: College Costs 73
Alex: Building Confidence...74
Rebecca: Connecting...75
All Students, All the Time..76

CHAPTER 8 Multimedia: LEARNING 24/7 78
Coherence Principle 79
Signaling Principle...80
Redundancy Principle 80
Spatial Contiguity Principle..80
Temporal Contiguity Principle 81
Segmenting Principle 81
Pre-Training Principle 81
Modality Principle 81
Multimedia Principle...81
Personalization Principle...82
Voice Principle 82
Image Principle 82

CHAPTER 9 COLLABORATIVE LEARNING: STUDENTS
HELPING STUDENTS 83
Collaborative Technologies 84

4

Wikis..84
The Google Suite 85
Blogs...85
Twitter...86
Classroom Games 86

CHAPTER 10 F2F TECHNOLOGY: MAKING IT CLICK 88
Integrating Technology **88**
Classroom Response System..88
Lecture Capture...90
PowerPoint...91
Digital Pens 91
Videos 92
Lab Hardware & Software **93**
Student Technology **94**

CHAPTER 11 STUDENT SELF-ASSESSMENT **96**
Before Class—Formative Assessment.................................**97**
During Class—More Formative Assessment **98**
After Class—Summative Assessment..................................**98**
The Dunning-Kruger Effect...**99**

CHAPTER 12 MEASURING INSTRUCTOR SUCCESS 101
Measuring The Success of Your Class................................**101**
Final Grades..102
Reflecting..102
Student Surveys 104
One Minute Notes 104
Student Evaluations 105
Engagement (Yours and Theirs)......................................**106**

PART IV BLENDING AT ANY LEVEL.......................108

CHAPTER 13 BLENDING LOWER-LEVEL, MID-LEVEL
AND UPPER-LEVEL SCIENCE COURSES **109**
Democratizing Science Through Blending **109**
Introductory Courses..**110**
Use Pre-Assessments...110
Technology for Introductory Courses....................................111
Blended General Chemistry I **113**
Class Time Management...**114**
Scaffolding..115

Peer Mentors 116
Homework & Quizzes **116**
Quizzes 117
Physics **119**
ConcepTests.. 120
Biology **121**
Mid-Level/Upper-Level Courses 123
The Focus on Cognitive Skills....................................... 123
Upper-Level Courses: Different But Similar 125

CHAPTER 14 COURSES FOR NON-MAJORS...................127
Teach Non-Majors Differently 127
Before, During and After 128
Before... 128
During: Biochemistry: Understanding the Bases of Human Disease 128
After—Astronomy.. 129

CHAPTER 15 BLENDED LABORATORY LEARNING.......131
Yes, You Can Blend Labs...**131**
Gross Anatomy 132

CHAPTER 16 PROFESSIONAL DEVELOPMENT:
GROWING AS A TEACHER.......................................136
Professional Organizations and Conferences 136
Journals 138
Teaching and Learning Centers................................ 139
Supporting Others 139

COPYRIGHT FAIR USE GUIDELINES FOR COLLEGE
FACULTY *141*
What Types of Creative Work Does Copyright Protect? 141
Permission: What Is It and Why Do I Need It? 141
Obtaining Clearance for Coursepacks 142
Using a Clearance Service.. 143
Educational Uses of Non-Coursepack Materials 143
The Code of Best Practices in Fair Use for Media
Literacy Education... 143
Guidelines Establish a Minimum, Not a Maximum.......... 144
What is the Difference Between the Guidelines and
Fair Use Principles?... 144
What is an "Educational Use?"....................................... 144

Rules for Reproducing Text Materials for Use in Class 145
Rules for Reproducing Music 145
Rules for Recording and Showing Television Programs 146

References **147**
Index **154**

Table of Figures

Figure 3.1—Bloom's Taxonomy 39
Figure 4.1—Learning Outcomes 45
Figure 5.1—Flipped and Blended Lesson Planning Template 54
Figure 8.1—Conceptualization of Multimedia Learning Theory
Adapted from Mayer 79
Figure 13.1—Lesson Schedule 114
Figure 13.2—Quiz Questions 117
Figure 13.3—Sample ConcepTest 120

Praise For *The Power of Blended Learning in the Sciences*

"At a time when the tools of technology can become the entire focus of blended course design, these authors have succeeded in placing the focus squarely where it belongs...on the learning. This book is a great resource that not only provides foundation and rationale for blended design, but specific and useful ideas about how to actually accomplish it! Both novice and experienced instructors will benefit from the book's suggestions for learner-centered strategies. In addition, this book's content is organized, understandable, and often makes the reader feel he/she is in a faculty development conversation with the authors. The reader comes away thinking 'Yes, I can do that!'"— *Vicky Morgan, Ph.D., Associate Dean Faculty Development Director, Teaching and Learning Center, College of Saint Mary*

"*The Power of Blended Learning in the Sciences* is a soup to nuts guide to everything you need to know about how to design courses in this format. The guiding theme of the book is that blended learning is not just another pedagogical fad, but rather an excellent framework for improving your teaching practice. While targeted for those who teach in the sciences, instructors in all disciplines will benefit from the accessible advice, well-structured format, and engaging writing. *The Power of Blended Learning* avoids the trap of being too theoretical or focused on technique. Readers learn the steps they need to blend their courses, why these steps are needed, and how they are in alignment with the science of learning. Both new teachers and tenured professors will find everything they need in this book to blend their course to improve student learning." *Christopher Price, Ph.D., Academic Programs Manager, SUNY Center for Professional Development*

"See Dick balance redox reactions. Balance, Dick, balance."

"Which competencies matter most for blended-learning teachers? Allison Powell, Beth Rabbitt, and Kathryn Kennedy, who authored the iNACOL Blended Learning Teacher Competency Framework, identified 'mindsets' as the first of four clusters of competencies that are important. 'Competency 1 Standard 1 for blended teachers,' according to an iNACOL report, is a mindset that reflects **a shift from teacher-led instruction to student-centered learning** for the purposes of meeting individual needs and fostering engagement and motivation."—*EDUCAUSE*

"The most successful blended learning teachers share these four mindset competencies: modeling a growth mindset; having an entrepreneurial, creative mindset; having a collaborative, teamwork mindset; and an openness-to-change mindset."—*Blended Learning Universe*

PREFACE: WHY BLEND SCIENCE INSTRUCTION?

Creating a blended science course takes time and energy. You need to plan at least six months ahead in order to fully design a successful course. Students may initially sneer at blended courses, and ask why instructors aren't teaching. Blended courses disrupt the centuries-old tradition of students learning at the feet of experts through the time-honored tradition of lecture, the Socratic Method.

Why then are we seeing such explosive growth in the number of blended courses across the educational landscape? Quite simply because blending creates more quality learning experiences than the de facto course design that characterizes today's teaching, i.e. the lecture. Blended courses integrate online resources which facilitate more active learning in the classroom. The blending of online activities outside the classroom combined with active learning strategies inside the classroom, catalyzes learning.

Society needs more scientifically literate people. We want a wider swath of students to understand more science and we want broader representation within science. Science education can improve—and blending is a great way to effect change. Blending can revolutionize science instruction through more effective, and more democratic, science education.

Concrete Reasons to Blend

1. Increased learning. Your students will learn more. The scholarly work (much of which is relatively new and much of which we explicate in the following chapters) continues to find that blending improves learning outcomes and that these outcomes endure well beyond the end of the term. Teachers sometimes forget that one of reasons to join this profession is to help others learn. Part of the job of a teacher is instill passion for a subject area and for learning.

We have had colleagues ask us why we they should make learning easy for students. "Aren't students supposed to struggle?" they ask. This makes no sense. Why wouldn't we want to increase efficiency of learning? When colleagues make snarky comments about lack of rigor, we let them know that blending improves learning outcomes without affecting rigor. As teachers, we want to grease the gears of learning to make it easier for students to turn the machinery that leads to learning. A lecture design has so much cognitive friction that lecturing impedes learning.

2. Less time in the classroom. Your students will learn more in a shorter time. College teachers, too often, do not look at the fixed nature of time. Does a three-credit course really need to meet for three hours each week? Students need to acquire knowledge and skills. The measure should be how much they learn not how much time they invest. A blended course that meets for one-third fewer hours than a traditional course saves approximately 15 hours/semester. In other words, the blended learning platform will save your students 15 hours of passive seat time. Saving time means increased efficiency as long as the learning outcomes are still met.

3. Evolution of a course. A pedagogically sound course design will make incremental change much easier. Blended courses evolve, because technology inevitably evolves as do students. A blended course, therefore, saves time over its life by being improved. The initial time and personal learning investment pay dividends, because subsequent course modification becomes less time consuming.

How many of us make the same error(s) on a subsequent course offering because we didn't correct the issue from the previous year? With a Master Course loaded on the LMS, new iterations of the course can be easily improved. You'll create a Master Course in your Learning Management System (LMS), set a template and this facilitates course evolution while archiving prior iterations. Course design elements such as correction of quiz answers, adding more questions from group discussions to the question pool, improved clarity of assignments based on student observation, better rubrics—all lead to even greater learning gains for students in future sections of the course.

Blending a course requires a significant investment of time. However, the time invested designing a blended course will improve learning, save time (yours and the students'), and allow you to become a more effective teacher over time. Despite these strong motivators many college teachers still lecture. Why? Inertia. Overcoming that inertia is critical to designing a blended course and to improving student success and faculty satisfaction.

Let's look at some reasons to reduce the amount of time you lecture—an important aspect of the blended learning platform.

Why Lecturing is Detrimental to Learning

By blending your science course you are choosing a more effective pedagogy than has ever before existed in higher education. You are turning away from a centuries-old paradigm. Instead of treating your students like scribes in a medieval monastery you are treating them like individual learners who can choose how they learn and, no, note taking is not what most of them will choose! Some students might still prefer notes but then we can direct them to the book, or perhaps our pre-class videos. You want to help students maximize their learning.

 When you think of teaching, think about what your students will *do*. Create exercises that allow them to interact with the material so that they will learn by *doing*.

Lecturing often seems to rely on a cult of personality. Let's face it, we are not all rock stars and students don't hang on our every word like the lyrics to their favorite song. In addition, there is increased competition in the modern classroom for attention. Regardless of syllabus policies, threats and cajoling by professors, students face multiple digital temptations to multi-task and that multi-tasking adversely impacts their attention spans. Students (and faculty) in the lecture-heavy learning environment fool themselves that there is robust learning when, in fact, students' concentration is severely compromised. The traditional lecture enables multi-tasking without initial consequences—those come later in the form of poor grades.

Why Blend?

When the poor grades arrive, students may not blame the digital attention thief, the "multi-tasker," because that culprit has long left the scene of the crime.

The impact of the compromised attention to the materials at hand only comes to light in evaluation settings. The learner stumbles through the exercise then wonders why s/he didn't do better: after the student "attended" every lecture. They confuse *attendance* with *attention.*

Blended learning environments are designed to keep the students on task and self-motivated. Openly or surreptitiously disappearing behind the glow of some LED screen is not possible when one must communicate, contribute, respond and think quickly. A blended course design brings active instruction and frequent formative assessment to the center of the educational experience for both the faculty member and the student. When they are in class, students are engaged in active learning.

 A meta-analysis of science classes revealed the astonishing finding that the lecture is so detrimental to student learning that it should no longer be studied as a control because any deviation from the lecture improves learning (Freeman et al., 2014). The traditional lecture-based approach is ineffective because the approach rests on the assumption that if the instructor tells students what to know, then the *instructor* has done all the work.

Relying primarily on lecture presumes that students are *tabulae rasae*, blank slates, a 17th-century theory popularized by the English philosopher John Locke in his "Essay Concerning Human Understanding" (1689). In fact, neurobiology has provided us with important evidence against the *tabula rasa* model. In Chapter 1 we delve into the neurobiology of learning and some evidence-based theories of how we can leverage human biology to greater learning efficiencies. We will focus on a modern conception of the brain and the science behind how our students learn and retain the information we teach them.

Contrary to what some newcomers think about blending, it is *not* simply a lecture placed online. Blending requires the pedagogical know-how to integrate the online activities with the Face-to-Face (F2F) active learning strategies. By altering your basal mindset about how teaching "looks" you'll soon find yourself with multiple roles that hardly resemble a traditional view of lecture-based teaching. Are you ready to take on this challenge? By shedding the preconception of what college teaching should look like you can help your students learn more. The curiosity that initially pulled you into your subject area can be reawakened. The excitement of trying something new will reignite you, your students, and your career.

 Blending a course requires you to think about your teaching in fundamentally different ways. You are no longer a "lecturer"; you are a "designer of learning experiences."

How to Blend

What does a course look like if there is no lecture? While a blended course reduces the amount time spent in the classroom, that reduction in time is not the reason to blend. Reducing the amount of time you spend in front of your students catalyzes a wholesale reconsideration of what it means to teach. Blending gives faculty the opportunity to reorganize a course around the idea that a teacher *facilitate* learning by structuring learning experiences inside *and* outside of class.

We all want students to think about our subject area outside of class. We might tell the class to "read the book prior to class" and to "study" after class. Such instructional strategies do not constitute good teaching. Students who receive more structured guidance about how to interact with the course material learn more effectively. The swim coach does not swim laps for his or her team, but instead creates workouts—in the pool, in the weight room, and in the swimmer's head. These forms of guidance keep the swimmer working toward constant improvement, goals and outcomes. When you teach, you are the coach creating learning activities linked to learning outcomes.

Why Blend?

To use another athletic analogy: Weight lifting produces poor results without appropriate time, load, variation and technique. A brain requires similar consideration. As a teacher, you understand the course content so well that you can invest time and energy to create effective "brain-lifting" routines for your students. You create workout routines to help your learners get cognitively stronger.

A blended design consists of three simple, but integrated parts: before, during, and after class. The depth of inquiry and knowledge increases each time the student revisits materials. Creating lesson plans that outline how and what your students will accomplish before, during and after class will help you shape your blended course and improve student learning outcomes.

Prior to Class:

This stage of the blending cycle sets the foundation for learning. Students might use a "Reading Guide" to help direct their pre-class reading. They could do a simple home experiment, watch a few short (less than 5 minutes) videos, or could take a quick field sample of some flora or fauna. You will provide detailed learning outcomes for every concept. Require students to complete a pre-class assignment related to the materials they prepared. The main purpose of pre-class work is to introduce students to course content, grease the cognitive wheels and get them thinking. We will call this step "prior knowledge" in later chapters.

During Class:

This stage of the blending cycle extends the pre-class learning and builds on the prior knowledge you introduced via the pre-class work. You've already introduced the content, now you want students to interact with the content. In class, the students take what they've learned and apply it. Students could be put into groups to collaboratively solve problems related to that the pre-class content. They might work collaboratively to examine a case study related to the content, complete a worksheet that helps them apply the content, or to answer a series of clicker questions.

Class time creates a space for students to learn from each other, as well as from the instructor. Regardless of the strategy employed, during this F2F stage, students need to be actively engaged with the content. Later chapters will develop this topic further. The mental activity of retrieving prior knowledge and appending new knowledge while organizing in meaningful ways or "schema" is very powerful (yet quite effortless to the learner).

A cautionary note: although students might not immediately "feel" as though they are learning, we would argue this is due to their classical conditioning of what demonstrates learning, a binder full of notes, printouts of the PowerPoint slides—archives of their attendance at the lectures. Slowly students in blended courses start to change their perceptions of what constitutes learning.

After Class:

The final phase of the blended learning cycle closes the loop and sets the stage for further learning. One goal after class is to provide rehearsal so their "comprehension blind spots" can be identified. Students might take an open-book, open-notes online quiz. Perhaps they have multiple attempts with only the highest score counting toward their grade. Ideally, after class ends the student is primed to deepen his/her knowledge. As their misconceptions are exposed, after-class assignments may be used to reach higher order learning goals, including evaluation and creation. As a high-level learning assignment, students could work on a project with multiple mileposts that you created to keep the learner on task.

To answer the question about how to blend, you'll need to think about what your students are doing when you aren't around. We know this suggestion can be humbling, because you want students to learn from *you*. In a blended course, a great deal of learning will occur when you aren't there…that's a good thing.

Which Kinds of Technology to Use

Possibly the most paralyzing decision you'll face is which kinds of technology to use. In our workshops, we are often confronted with teachers concerned that they are using "wrong" technology. Let's make this clear up front: there is no perfect technology. Technology is a tool you will use at your own pace, and with your own persona, to help your pedagogic task. By all means explore different types of technology. Listen to student feedback about how to improve your use of technology. Be willing to learn how to use different technology. But remember: there is not one technological solution for your courses. We will present you with many types of technological tools, but ultimately you should focus on your pedagogy. What do you want your students to learn and how will technology help?

One of the most dramatic changes in technology comes in the form of mobile devices. We once had a workshop participant say that they make their students drop off their cell phones at the classroom door. While the insistence came from a good place, it implies that the educator was acting like the sage on the stage, demanding the attention of their students and imposing a top down structure in the class. When a syllabus includes a ten-point grade deduction when students look at a cell phone, the instructor has already lost sight of the point of teaching. We encourage you to integrate mobile technology. Tell your students to get out their mobile devices as their phones will help them develop better questions, answers, and discussion inputs. See how blending simply does not align with traditional classroom interactions? A 2016 EDUCAUSE student survey contained the following recommendation:

Faculty need to overcome their reservations about harnessing student technologies, especially mobile devices, for academic work in the classroom. This can be accomplished by engaging in skillful, thoughtful, and effective uses of technology in the classroom that are grounded in empirical research that demonstrates benefits to students. Faculty can also seek direct assistance from instructional designers to design and/or redesign assignments and courses, and take advantage of technology-oriented professional development opportunities (Brooks, 2016).

 The same survey found that 82 percent of students surveyed preferred a blended learning environment (Brooks, 2016). When each of us started blending we were met with resistance from students and colleagues: students wanted lecturing because they were used to that form of teaching (and it allowed them be more passive learners) and colleagues thought we were shirking responsibility. The survey results demonstrate that blending is here to stay in large part because your students will prefer it; very soon students will expect it.

Why Not Blend?

We prefaced this book by outlining the positive aspects of blended learning for both the faculty member and the student. However, rather than asking why an instructor should blend her/his course, perhaps the better question is "Why not?!?" Whether you are a tenured professor teaching one or two courses per year or an adjunct teaching a plethora of classes, blended course design and instruction offer you a proven approach to improve student outcomes, according to the results of recent studies.

- Blended design improves learning.

- Blended design can be fun for you.

- Blended design allows you to evolve your courses based on student feedback and outcomes.

- Blended design will help you evolve professionally to become an even more skilled and effective instructor.

This book will take you step-by-step through the process to create a blended science course no matter which discipline you teach in or what type of course—including labs—that you teach. We will start by discussing the how and what behind the physiological learning process and you will see how blended learning dovetails with the brain's process of learning, retaining the synthesizing information.

We'll entertain you with anecdotes, and we'll share our successful and unsuccessful blended course design experiences. In this book, we'll show you how to design, create and facilitate blended science courses in any discipline that significantly improve learning outcomes and boost instructor satisfaction.

Happy Reading,

Tim, Ollie and Ike

How To Get the Most Out of This Book

Did you notice the use of these icons in the preface to this book? An important tool in this book is the use of icons to high-light important information for the reader.

Keys to Success: Whenever you see this icon, you'll want to take special note. These are tried and true tips, concepts and ideas to help you blend your courses.

Caution Light: Whenever you see this icon, you'll know what others who have successfully blended their classes have discovered NOT to do while planning and teaching their courses.

In addition to the icons, the table of contents is very detailed to get you to the topic that most interests you at the moment. An index has been compiled for ease of use. Finally, at the end of this book, there is a detailed section that deals with copyright guidelines for college faculty.

This book is your detailed reference for blended learning in the sciences. Use this book as a manual, a guide, or for professional reading. It contains practical and informative strategies to assist you. It is written in a user-friendly manner for your convenience. Enjoy it and GOOD TEACHING.

Part I

Reasons to Blend

CHAPTER 1
NEUROBIOLOGY PRIMER: THE THINK ORGAN

As an educator, you want to change the way people think. You need to understand how students think and need to find ways to better understand student thinking. But what is thinking? What does thinking look like? In order to explore thinking, we'll start with a tour of the thing that allows us to think.

The Thinking Organ

Let's start with overall anatomy. The brain is a delicate jelly-like organ floating in a fluid-filled cranium. The cerebral cortex is the outmost layer of cells on the corrugated surface of the brain. When you look at a brain and see the hills and valleys you are actually seeing the outer layer of cells. This outer peel of cells called the cortex is often what we think of as "brain cells". The thin layer consists of the cell bodies of working neurons, devouring glucose and using more oxygen than other tissues ten times its weight. Don't be fooled by the brain's lack of volume: the cortex contains billions of interconnected neurons.

The cortex is just part of the story, because a single brain cell cannot do much by itself; it takes a noisy community of brain cells to get even the simplest jobs done. To put it simply, neurons essentially yell across a crevasse at each other. Their language is both electrical and chemical in nature and it occurs at blazing speeds, usually in one direction. An ionic wave of electrical current, called a depolarization wave, streaks down the long appendage (axon) of a nerve cell. When the wave reaches the end of the line it crashes on the shore. The wave can't jump the crevasse. The cleft between neurons is called the synapse and the nerve cell formulates a recipe of chemicals called neurotransmitters that it spews out into the synapse when the electrical wave crashes on the shore. The neurotransmitters spill into the crevasse and reach other neurons. Imagine yourself calling across a small valley to your hiking partner in a popular park: do you think your partner will be the only person hearing your call? This is how one neuron firing can then speak to many more neurons through amplification.

The brain cells must connect to each other but the brain must connect to the senses in order to gather information about the world. Sense information helps facilitate learning. We must remember some of what we sense which is why memory is so important. Without memory, learning can't happen. Learning does not involve new neuron formation. Instead the connections between neurons strengthen. The brain responds to learning by replicating more neurotransmitters, changing its recipe of the neurotransmitters, slowing the breakdown of older transmitters, and adjusting the gains on the receivers for these neurotransmitters to make memories more vivid or perhaps to allow the less used information to be less accessible.

Neuronal Anatomy

We'd like to help you understand how your students' brains operate. Think of yourself as the proverbial fly on the wall right now. This wall, however, is not the wall of a room. Your perspective is too grand: shrink down and position yourself on the axon of a single brain cell in the gray matter. Axons are positioned vertically. The axon resembles a tube stretching upwards to the edge of the grey matter and downwards into the brain and the white matter there. The axon is rumbling inside as rivulets of fluid move to support the energy and repair demands of the cell: it quakes slightly as it lives, respires, and excretes just as the human that carries it. You can see fast and periodic waves of gated channels, essentially one way doors, opening and closing quickly as this nerve cell conducts the electrical current in a one way direction.

You have a great vantage here: surrounding your gray matter look-out post are innumerable other axons stretching out like a massive forest around you. Hello? You can overhear and understand their language! If you look up, you see the underside of the skull through the cloudy layers that make the brain and skull waterproof. You can hear and feel the owner's heartbeat as this sound reverberates in the cerebrospinal fluid. You also feel the circulatory pressure waves generated in the cerebrospinal fluid. They might resemble a rhythmic breeze. As you look downward, millions of white matter cells come into focus. Their branch-like dendritic arms make wavy tracts they streak away in many directions beyond view. Although you can see a good distance from your vantage, it is by no means a calm place.

The neurobiology of your brain is messy and doesn't resemble the organized diagrams of our textbooks. There are currents pushing and pulling, ionic lightning storms, wafts of cellular respiration gases, and if you squint, you can see rain showers of little bubbles moving between the innumerable and multiplying synaptic clefts everywhere. The bubbles are vesicles full of neurotransmitters. At a basic level, the vesicular traffic takes the form of neuronal Morse code that scientists are only starting to understand at a cell-to-cell level. In this imaginary vantage point, brain cells are not simply "off" or "on." The intrinsic meteorology is vastly influenced by the overall health of the system, the mood of the owner, by diet, and by drugs. Your emotions that particular day matter. Your ingestion of drugs—whether caffeine (your 3rd cup of coffee for the day) or prescription drugs that have side-effects—matter. Multiple factors influence our readiness and willingness to pay attention or engage, and that ladies and gentlemen, is directly related to neurotransmission.

Your goal is to help students tap into their own neurochemistry with as little effort as possible. Work with biology, not against it.

We now have an appreciation of the raging biology that is occurring within our crania which enable "outside" stimuli to get in our heads. But how does it happen? One proviso is that science is still learning about what learning looks like neurobiologically, but we do know some things. When you learn something new (a fact, a technique, the name of a scholar) you ignite a set of synapses that expend energy to get that memory to stick. Once that memory is slightly sticky, the chances of making that neural network work again increases. Biologically, this might mean that neurons are potentiated and just waiting to get the Morse code of neurotransmission release from their neighbors to then up the volume of their own voice. This potentiation effect strengthens with experience so yes, doing those math problems at the end of the chapter did help strengthen some of the neural networks associated with the particular quadratic equations at hand. The yang to this yin is that there are inhibitory effects. Inhibitory processes will disable, de-tune, demodulate, or just simmer down neurons that are connected to the neural network that are *not* useful to that particular skill set. Regardless of the mechanism or neurotransmitter involved, the framework of neurons that you see as a fly on the wall are biological representations of experiences in our lives, some of which occur in school and that we call learning in the formal sense.

The brain looks after itself. It cannot make new neurons so it maintains them in their original condition whenever possible. The brain renews what it can, drawing upon its own DNA design to maintain intrinsic organelles the way your uncle keeps the upholstery clean, repair/replace surface channels like the uncle would the spark plugs, and replacing membrane channels is like your uncle waxing his car. The brain even responds to learning by either replicating more neurotransmitters, changing its recipe of the neurotransmitters, slowing the breakdown of older transmitters, and adjusting the gains on the receivers for these neurotransmitters.

With this newly formed perspective of the messy inner workings of our think organ we can perhaps explore how to take better advantage of neuronal communication providing thoughtful ameliorations and steer clear of roadblocks. We need to encourage synaptic formation, organization, and endurance. We should enable synapses to organize into enduring schema. And we should reduce cognitive load.

Reducing Cognitive Load

As teachers, we want to make learning easier: that's our role as educators. As we cautioned in the introduction, this view of "easy" learning is not shared by all teachers. When a teacher tries to make learning easier, however, there is a lot of baggage to unpack. One trouble is that we often fall into the trap of teaching in the same way we were taught. That may stunt our students' growth as learners. Currently, science has not yet defined the edges of human long-term memory. We do, however, have a clear-eyed understanding of the limits of short-term (or working) memory. Information in working memory has but seconds to organize up to nine items into a meaningful context that can be committed to long-term memory. We try to help our learners move information into long-term memory through our actions as teachers: our role in designing blended classes is really trying to find a way to help students move information into long-term memory.

How do we help students commit information to long-term memory? Voluminous research indicates that we need to activate two major sensory channels in the learner: the eyes and the ears. By making some relatively simple changes in the way you teach, the task of learning simply becomes easier. You want to help students build long-term memory and 'there's a theory for that.'

The theory is called cognitive load. Reduction of cognitive load can occur through better instructional design. When cognitive load is reduced, learning is easier. While there is such a things as a 'desirable difficulty' too often teachers unwittingly add difficulty that is not desirable. Challenging students is one thing but confusing them is another. Three types of cognitive load have been identified: extraneous, germane, and intrinsic.

Extraneous load is a load that you, as a teacher, can reduce. Extraneous load can be reduced through better organization, clearer questions, and concise explanations. Blended design should ideally reduce extraneous load to almost zero. Intrinsic cognitive load is a load that you have no control over. Intrinsic load is related primarily to the difficulty inherent in the discipline. Intrinsic load is different for different learners: Tim finds organic chemistry utterly confounding but can speak several languages while Ike finds organic chemistry rather easy but has been unable to learn a second language. Germane load is individualized to the student. Diet, restfulness, health, family, state of mind, and love life all affect a learner's germane load. Your goal as a teacher is to try to work with that germane load to motivate your learners.

The only type of cognitive load that you can affect is the *extraneous* cognitive load. Try to eliminate it.

Multimedia Learning

The theory of multimedia learning is set on three underlying theories: the dual channel, limited capacity, and active processing theories. In the previous paragraphs we've described the general neural biology that underpins active processing and the energy required to make it happen. We've also spoken to the limited desktop of our working memory and how fleeting it is. One thing that wasn't discussed earlier is the idea of reception: getting information about our outside world into our brains not just to experience it but to make sense of it and to respond to it. Since multimedia learning theory speaks to the eyes and ears as their dual channels, let's highlight just a little of their neurobiological features supporting them. By the way, sight and sound are but two channels of sensory inputs including taste, smell, and touch.

The Dual Channel theory contends that we learn with our eyes and ears: both senses are important but process information through entirely separate sensory channels. Each sense uses different sensing equipment, wiring, and areas of our brains to get their jobs done. In your teaching, if you do more than pure oration from behind a screen or you are a pure mime, you are using different media—multimedia.

 Reading PowerPoint slides does not count as activating eyes and ears. You will add extraneous load because your eyes process written and spoken words differently.

Regardless of the wiring and connectivity, Mayer and many others have tested each sensory pathway separately and together. Mayer's studies have found significant learning improvements when the pathways are combined to effectively "instruct" learners. Mayer's model of multimedia learning theory incorporates the two channels of sensory input, working memory, and the potential to get information more easily to long-term memory. We will cover more about multimedia in Chapter 8. For now suffice it to say that when you find ways to engage your students' eyes and ears you will increase the amount of information your students will learn.

CHAPTER 2
EFFECTIVELY TEACHING WHAT YOU KNOW

Where Do I Start?

In Chapter 3, we'll jump into the how-to's of blended learning. Before we do that, however, let's discuss the basics of good teaching. A perfectly blended course won't produce improved student outcomes unless the instructor implements teaching best practices. Increased teacher satisfaction comes with being open to learning about and integrating instructional change.

The three of us have been involved in many different professional development initiatives. Whether it's instructing faculty on using Web 2.0 technologies with their students, or providing guidance with teaching with iPads, or helping faculty set up online classes, we try to inspire and challenge our colleagues to take risks and try new instructional methods. Regardless of the venue or the topic, the conversation always leads to the same question: "Where do I start?"

"Where do I start?" is not just about beginnings. In its essence, the question signals the apprehension of tackling something new and perhaps difficult. "Where do I start?" is about seeing a mountain in the distance and knowing that the journey is going to be a challenge. So, instead of providing a specific starting point, we've adopted a more Taoist approach to answering the question: Start with one.

Taken from a quote credited to Confucius and Lao Tzu, "start with one" channels the basic idea that any long journey begins with that first step. So take it. Start walking.

Instructional change is a journey of 1000 miles, but don't get caught up in the magnitude of it all. Start slowly and focus on making one change. For example, pick one lesson in which to embed some new technology or in which you will adopt some new instructional approach. When you start to blend your courses, don't change your entire course load. Start with one course, then pick one lesson or a lab. Don't worry about the 1,000 miles ahead of you. Just take that first step. Then take another and another. After a while, those 1,000 miles won't seem so overwhelming.

At times, the road will be a little bumpy. Focus on evaluating your progress. We explain to workshop participants that perfection shouldn't be the goal right out of the blocks. Instead, focus on being effective and work from there. We've all developed lessons that were train wrecks from some point of view yet were still effective in helping our students learn. Strive for effectiveness first and then worry about perfection later.

Now that we know how the brain processes and stores information—how our students' brains work as they strive to master course content—let's turn to teaching.

Teaching Best Practices

Teaching science is a challenging job. When you walk into a classroom, you are greeted by students with different life experiences, different academic abilities and different goals and motivations. Despite these vast differences, you are expected to generate uniform learning so that all students can achieve at comparable levels. To reach parity, you must perform a complicated dance that draws on each student's background knowledge, introduces experiences to build new knowledge and facilitates opportunities for student reflection and broader application. There are many synchronized moving pieces required to help a class of students learn a new concept.

Take into account the different experiences your students bring with them into your classroom. Leave time in class to walk around the class to talk to your students while they are working on something related to the course. By interacting with students, gathering information about them, their learning styles, you will be a more effective teacher.

Be a Content Expert—Teach What You Know

To navigate the complicated terrain of a collegiate classroom, what do you need to know to effectively teach? Instructors need to be content experts. A teacher who doesn't have a strong foundation in her/his content area can't effectively teach it. Please don't confuse a momentary lack of confidence with a lack of content knowledge; every faculty member experiences the "imposter syndrome," where we might question our skills, abilities and reasons for teaching.

For example, while each of the authors of this book has an extensive background in science, our individual knowledge bases are discipline specific: one of us has expertise in chemistry, another in physics, and the third in neuroanatomy. Despite our individual content expertise, however, we couldn't easily switch our teaching assignments, because we would be imposters. A background in neuroscience doesn't mean that Tim could effectively teach organic chemistry. Despite having a degree in physics, Ollie couldn't teach anatomy and physiology. Faculty need to be expert in their subject matter to teach it.

That being said, subject matter knowledge is not the only ingredient needed for successful teaching. Despite best intentions and a content-specific knowledge base, the ineffective teacher does not facilitate learning. Think back to your own courses as a college student. You had some credentialled instructor whose teaching was simply ineffective:

- The faculty member didn't interact with students;

- The faculty member didn't recognize when students struggled with material or how to structure content to foster growth;

- The faculty member breezed over challenging concepts so quickly that it was hard to keep up.

The difference between a content expert and a good teacher has been described this way: "Expertise in a particular domain does not guarantee that one is good at helping others learn it. In fact, expertise can sometimes hurt teaching because many experts forget what is easy and what is difficult for students (Bransford, 2000)."

Content knowledge is a critical ingredient for effective teaching, but other ingredients are equally important. Examining the knowledge base of teachers, Shulman (1986) proposed different intersecting knowledge bases that were required for effective instruction. Besides content knowledge and an understanding of general teaching strategies, Shulman argued to support student learning, instructors also need pedagogical content knowledge (PCK).

Pedagogical Content Knowledge (PCK)

PCK is, in fact, critical: while teaching requires that we know our field (content knowledge) and general teaching strategies (pedagogical knowledge), we must also know discipline-specific teaching strategies. PKC emerges from five distinct areas (Magnusson et al., 1999):

1. orientation with respect to teaching

2. knowledge of the curriculum

3. knowledge of the testing of knowledge

4. knowledge about learners

5. knowledge about strategies of passing on knowledge

How is PCK learned? Many professors acquire PCK through pedagogical modeling: they teach the way they were taught. This has been described as the "apprenticeship of observation (Lortie, 2002)." When we were students each of us experienced the teaching strategies of our respective fields. Ike saw how chemistry teachers taught. Ollie experienced what a physics classroom looked like. Through our years as students in our content areas, we were apprenticed into teaching (and learning) that subject. While apprenticeship is a powerful means of training, the model has some powerful downsides in the college classroom.

First, many of us came up through traditional lecture-based classrooms which modeled lecture as the primary means of teaching. Recent research shows that lecturing is ineffective for the broader student population.

Let's take a closer look at the study on classrooms that we referenced in the Preface. Compiling data from 225 different studies on active learning in Science, Technology, Engineering and Mathematics (STEM) related courses, the researchers found that students in lecture-based courses were 1.5 times more likely to fail than students in classes that utilized active learning. Across the studies, the average failure rates were 21.8 percent in classes that employed active learning and 33.8 percent in traditional lecture classroom environments.

How compelling was the analysis to the researchers? Since they were traditionally trained scientists, they communicated their findings in language that other scientists would understand. If the experiments analyzed here had been conducted as randomized controlled trials of medical interventions, they may have been stopped for benefit—meaning that enrolling patients in the control condition might be discontinued because the treatment being tested was clearly more beneficial (Freeman et al., 2014). If lecture-based instruction were the primary model for you as a student, your PCK is likely to be colored by this apprenticeship.

Trying to teach the way you were taught puts *you* at the center of learning, not your students.

Another challenge with the apprenticeship of observation is that it doesn't readily teach other critical areas of PCK. Take "knowledge of students" for example. As experts in our field, we may not have experienced the difficulty that our students face when learning a concept. Our science students come to our classrooms with "alternative frameworks" that are difficult to overcome.

Students cannot be thought of as empty containers to be loaded with the knowledge, but rather students are rich with experience, knowledge and the beliefs of their own understanding of the phenomena that occur in nature (Seligin, 2012). Students already have the scientific knowledge acquired from the environment, interaction with parents and friends, media, culture and socialization factors in which one concept is usually related directly to the students' understanding related to the environment (Joel K. Abraham et. al.,

2009). Before learning occurs, students already have their views and opinions of different explanations as recommended by scientists (Osborne et. al.., 1983).

Here's an example of PCK from physics: when a heavy object and a light object fall simultaneously from same height, which object strikes the ground first? You may remember that gravity acts on heavy objects and light objects the same way. Since they're dropped from the same height at the same time, they'll hit the ground simultaneously. The challenge with this example is that most physics students can shout out the answer in class. Providing this example in a lecture format doesn't challenge students' existing beliefs.

Changing the situation and instructional format, however, will elicit some interesting answers from students. For instance, what would happen if someone shot a gun horizontally and dropped a bullet from the same height as the gun's muzzle? Which would hit the ground first? Offering this example for students to discuss in small groups leads to creative explanations. While students can parrot the right answer when asked a gravitational question in a straightforward way, more complex examples will expose their alternative frameworks of how gravity acts on objects.

Despite sitting through numerous lessons on how gravity works, some physics students may never fully confront the content if taught through lecture. Students need to have their belief systems challenged. By offering perplexing examples, students move from simply repeating a programmed response to reflective thinking. The learner must directly confront his or her alternative framework.

Where do these "alternative frameworks" come from? As we mentioned in the last chapter, students do not come to our classrooms as blank slates. They've had a multitude of experiences that have informed their understanding of the world. They may have seen a piece of paper falling more slowly than a baseball, for instance, or a leaf fall at a constant speed from a tree. With the number of situations where heavy objects and light objects hit the ground at different times in everyday life, it's not surprising to see this as a common misunderstanding among students. While this is a single physics example, these alternative frameworks are pervasive across the sciences.

In the 1993 documentary titled "A Private Universe," an interviewer asks college graduates to explain how seasons change (Sadler et al., 1989). Despite emerging moments earlier from their commencement ceremonies, many were unable to accurately explain how seasons occurred on the Earth. The students possessed alternative frameworks that were hard to break, despite years of instruction.

Let's return to PCK. How do these "alternative frameworks" relate to a faculty member's pedagogical content knowledge? To be effective, instructors must understand their students' prior knowledge and the alternative frameworks they possess. Such information isn't easily acquired during an "apprenticeship of observation." While this is just one aspect of PCK, it demonstrates the complex nature of teaching science and the difficulty with developing PCK among faculty.

Cartoonstock.com

You may have read other books about teaching strategies or attended a workshop on how to be a better teacher. You may been left feeling like you didn't really know how to implement the strategies in your own classroom. While books and workshops may be helpful at developing general pedagogical knowledge, they may not always be as effective in developing discipline-specific pedagogical content knowledge. Developing science PCK is one of the motivations that led to writing this book. While there are numerous books that explore how to blend collegiate classes, few explore the unique nature, benefits and challenges of blending science classes.

Since our focus is blending, it's important to discuss another knowledge base that's critical for instructors. Many faculty new to blended instruction recognize that they have to develop some technological knowledge to be successful. Maybe they need to learn how screencast or develop online quizzes, or how to use clickers. While we'll explore all of these tools, general technological knowledge is as helpful as general pedagogical knowledge: it can only get an instructor so far. Instead of examining technology generally, we must examine how technology can be used specifically to teach content. Just as there is PKC there is also TPACK (Technological Pedagogical Content Knowledge) (Mishra and Koehler, 2006).

By taking a disciplinary focus on blending, we'll develop in readers the pedagogical content knowledge to successfully change classroom environments. The strategies, examples and technologies we share will develop TPACK, as well. As developers of TPACK have written: "Teaching with technology is a difficult thing to do well. TPACK... suggests that content, pedagogy, technology, and teaching/learning contexts have roles to play individually and together. Teaching successfully with technology requires continually creating, maintaining, and re-establishing a dynamic equilibrium among all components" (Mishra and Koehler, 2006).

Creating a blended science classroom requires instructors to navigate these individual components and successfully balance each in support of their students' development.

CHAPTER 3
BLENDING: GIMME A "B..."

Thus far we've examined the thinking organ and explored why being a subject expert does not automatically translate to being a great teacher. Now it's time to start digging into why blending a course helps learners and why you need to understand both your content and pedagogy.

Let's establish up front that there's no one right way to blend. To design a blended class, you need to consider a variety of factors including the content you'll be teaching, the students with whom you'll be working, your institution's level of commitment for blended instruction and its capacity to support online and face-to-face instruction. This chapter is intended to provide an overview of the pedagogical foundations for blended learning to better equip you to make informed decisions as you design your courses.

What's in a Name?

While "blended learning" sounds like a straightforward term, it is actually commonly used to describe a wide expanse of instructional practices from K-12 to college. The overuse of the term causes confusion as to what really counts as a blended course: "there are many forms of blended...[but] a generally accepted taxonomy does not exist. One school's blended is another school's hybrid, or another school's mixed-mode (Picciano et al., 2007)." In the K-12 arena, terms such as flex learning, flipped learning and personalized learning all fall under the larger umbrella of blended learning. While the K-12 grouping is useful in fostering innovation, the classification system does not reflect the types of blended learning occurring in collegiate environments.

The way we to use the term—and probably the most widely held view—is that a blended course contains a combination of online and face-to-face modes to support student learning with some reduction in the amount of class time. Most institutions of higher education categorize blended courses as those where "substantial proportion of the content is delivered online, typically uses online discussions, and typically has a reduced number of face-to-face meetings (Allen, et. al., 2016)." A "substantial proportion" usually means any reduction from 30-79 percent of the content is delivered through online means. Focusing on reduction of in-class instruction time does not fully capture how the online and face-to-face environments are used to support student learning.

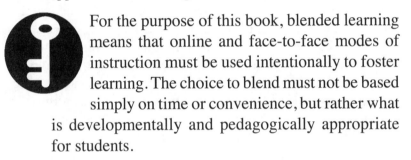 For the purpose of this book, blended learning means that online and face-to-face modes of instruction must be used intentionally to foster learning. The choice to blend must not be based simply on time or convenience, but rather what is developmentally and pedagogically appropriate for students.

For example, you shouldn't plan an online component if you're simply going to miss a day of class. Online and face-to-face environments should be used purposefully to scaffold students' content and conceptual development and strategically, with a clear understanding of instructional goals for each component of the course. When you blend you fuse online with face-to-face environments you'll create a seamless course that is better then either environment on its own.

Our view of blended learning involves moving the majority of content delivery online so that you almost completely eliminate the need to lecture. You'll use the face-to-face environment to support student engagement and higher-level learning. This view of blended learning is best captured with the following acronym:

B - Balanced

L - Learner-Centered

E - Engagement-Driven

N - Novel

D - Dynamic

In the following sections, we'll examine each of these descriptors in depth and how these apply to blended course design.

B-Balanced

In blended classes, instructors must balance the use of online and face-to-face environments and consider which environment is appropriate for their instructional goals. A long-time Biology teacher has expressed this concern: "one danger in redesigning a face-to-face course to the blended mode is that online exercises are simply added to the existing face-to-face activities without regard to how online and face-to-face learning will work together (Bergtrom, 2011)." Consider the differences between virtual and physical learning environments. Students usually navigate virtual learning environments individually while they rarely occupy a physical classroom on their own. While learning management systems are beginning to support more video and audio involvement from students, interaction is still largely based on text-based communication. As the majority of online interaction occurs asynchronously, face-to-face interaction is always synchronous. Such differences afford different instructional benefits for students. For instance, online environments are ideal for content delivery, for low stakes assessment and for discussion forums that support asynchronous interaction amongst students and faculty.

While all of these activities are essential for student learning, the face-to-face environment can extend student interaction, collaboration, and engagement. Face-to-face environments are ideal for building classroom community and for group problem solving opportunities. Effective blending requires balancing the use of these environments to offer a broader learning experience for students than either environment would offer on its own. **An instructor who uses face-to-face class time primarily for high stakes summative assessment is not balancing their instruction purposefully.**

While the face-to-face environment allows easy proctoring of assessments (like exams), the setting also offers significant instructional benefits. Learning is a social act. Students learn by interacting with their peers. While interaction can be achieved through online means, it is more easily built in physical classroom spaces. To develop an effective blended class, you must balance the social physical space with the independence offered online.

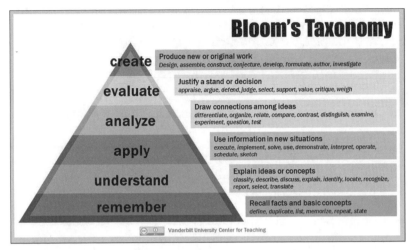

Figure 3.1: Bloom's Taxonomy

L-Learner-Centered

Effective blended classes focus on the instructional needs of the learner. Teachers must therefore consider the overall learning objectives they hope to achieve and how best to scaffold students to meet these objectives. We recommend examining the levels of learning offered in Bloom's Taxonomy (above) to intentionally build higher levels of thinking during class time. Knowledge and comprehension of course content can be effectively supported through the use of recorded lessons, videos, tutorials and simulations. Pre-class content knowledge provides the instructional foundation for higher order learning that happens in class. While gathered as a whole class in physical space, students start to apply the knowledge to new situations and to use their understanding to analyze data or case studies. After class, students are now better equipped to do higher order evaluation and synthesis on their own. The three-tiered approach of before, during, and after class provides a scaffolded approach to learning that focuses on the developmental trajectories of students. Effective blended learning puts the needs of the learner at the center of instructional decision-making and planning. The next three chapters will explore each aspect of this three-tiered approach.

E-Engagement-Driven

While blended classes can offer students independence because of the online components of a course you must keep student engagement in mind as you plan courses (Bergmann and Sams, 2007). A good guide for fostering student engagement is The Seven Principles for Good Practice in Undergraduate Education (Chickering and Gamson, 1987).

1. Encourage contact between students and faculty

2. Develop reciprocity and cooperation among students

3. Encourage active learning

4. Give prompt feedback

5. Emphasize time on task

6. Communicate high expectations

7. Respect diverse talents and ways of learning

While these principles were written long before blended learning emerged in institutions of higher education, they still offer a sound guide for fostering student engagement in blended courses. While any of these principles can be established in either the online or face-to-face portions of a blended class, some are better suited for certain modes. For instance, while active learning can be accomplished online, face-to-face settings offer a better location for the type of social interaction that is at the heart of active learning strategies. Being engagement-driven means considering how the different environments can be effectively used to involve students in the learning process.

N-Novel

Although blended learning can be considered a novel approach at many institutions, we are using the term more to describe the changing roles of students and instructors. In traditional lecture-based classrooms, the instructor actively presented content while the students passively received this instruction. A blended class, however, presents novel roles for both instructor and student. In a blended class, the instructor takes on new roles as both a designer and facilitator of learning. The student's role also changes in this process. When they're navigating the online portions of the a blended class, the student must take on the role of independent and motivated learner. In the face-to-face portions, however, their roles can also incorporate active learner and collaborator. By changing how, when and where learning happens, blended learning offers novel roles for both instructor and students.

D-Data-Driven

As you design your blended course, keep in mind that the structure should evolve according to students' needs. The dynamic (another "D") nature of blended classes is driven by assessment of student learning. In a way, assessments act as a compass to guide the overall implementation of a blended class. As students progress through the different online and face-to-face phases of a blended learning cycle, instructors should assess student learning and use that data to inform their plans and change directions as needed.

As teachers, we tend to focus on what our students are learning from us. We also need to consider what we're learning from our students. As you examine students' formative assessment data, be prepared to adapt instructional plans to meet their needs. For instance, while we advocate for using the face-to-face time for active learning opportunities, micro-lessons may be needed depending on the assessment data we obtain. By spanning both online and face-to-face environments, blended classes offer a dynamic model for tailoring instruction to meet students' needs.

Self-Study Questions for Blended Design

B Balanced:

How am I planning to use the online and face-to-face environments to support student learning? How can I balance the environments to best support my students?

L Learner-centered:

How can I structure my instruction to scaffold my students' learning? How can I effectively build understanding prior to students attending face-to-face classes?

E Engagement-driven:

How can I engage students during the online and face-to-face portions of my class? What active learning strategies can I use to encourage interaction and cooperation amongst students?

N Novel:

Am I prepared to adopt new instructional roles in my class? How can I support students to adopt their new roles?

D Data-Driven:

How can I collect formative assessment data at different points of a blended learning cycle? Am I prepared to change directions to meet my students' needs?

Part II
The Blended Cycle

CHAPTER 4
BLENDING—WHEN STUDENTS LEARN WITHOUT YOU

Students can learn before you ever interact with them. As counter-intuitive as this may seem, students are capable of learning without you around. Admitting this to yourself can create some psychological turmoil. You may have to create a mantra to remind yourself that they can learn without you, but then you might wonder if you will soon be out of a job. Rest assured. Students need you. The instructor of the 21st century risks having students vote with their feet if the instructor refuses to consider creative ways to engage students prior to class.

Your job is to help students start thinking about content before they come to class. You may think that your role is to disseminate information and in that you would not be alone. A survey of more than 700 faculty found that more than half reported lecturing in every one of their last ten class sessions (Smith and Valentine, 2012). Unfortunately if you believe that only you control the content, then the sobering conclusion is that no learning can occur prior to class. In the "Instruction Paradigm" (Barr and Tagg, 1995a) the teacher is center stage: "learning is teacher-centered and controlled" and "knowledge comes in 'chunks' and 'bits' delivered by instructors." In such a paradigm little time is spent thinking about what students could learn prior to class because the teacher is not present prior to class.

 Design your course with pre-class work in mind. Students are more capable than you think. Give them clear, concise directions and then expect that they will complete the assigned work.

Someone who follows the instruction paradigm might assign a chapter before class but then will proceed to teach as if no student had completed the reading. The lecture is usually about what the student should have gotten from the reading. A diligent student who invests significant time preparing for class by completing the reading will quickly learn that they do not need to invest such time prior to class because the instructor will summarize the content more effectively than the student would be able to do.

In the instruction paradigm the role of the teacher is to provide/deliver content. A blended design helps circumvent the limitations of the transmission model. You want to help motivate student learning prior to class so that students can construct their own understanding of the content. Even if you are committed to an instructional paradigm, you can alter when and where transmission of knowledge occurs. Your fears about the quality of student learning prior to class are understandable.

Over and over in workshops, faculty reveal that their reservations about interactive teaching stem not so much from their unwillingness to be effective teachers or engage their students in meaningful ways as from their fear that these methods will exact time they don't have or time they need to produce the research that largely determines professional mobility, salary, and prestige. In this framework, teaching well and saving time seem totally contradictory. [We] suggest that the way out of the dilemma is to move first exposure to student's own time (Walvoord and Pool, 1998).

Organization

The first job you have is to organize your course. Use the LMS to create Modules for each day, each week, or each topic. Each module should include the resources that the learner will need including: learning goals, pre-class assignments, videos, PowerPoints, worksheets, and assessments, such as quizzes. The goal is to create a single source of information to help the learner interact with the content. You want to create an ergonomic LMS design. Students should have a single splash page that they see where they can easily link to each aspect of the module.

In this section we focus on the pre-class work. What do want students to do before they ever see you? Keep in mind that you need to create activities that are self-explanatory because the students will working on their own time. The most critical aspect of the pre-class work is clearly written Learning Outcomes.

Learning Outcomes

You must include Learning Outcomes (LOs) for every module: "By the end of this module students will be able to …" In our workshops, participants inevitably grumble that they already have LOs. Administrators require them because accrediting agencies require them. The exercise of working with LOs may seem like bureaucratic excess. It is not. You need to learn how to use LOs to direct student learning. You may need to help educate your students about using LOs effectively so they can maximize the potential of LOs. The LOs should be the first thing a student reads online, because they must use the LOs to guide their studying.

Outcomes like the ones listed in the first column below are too generic and are not useful to students. Be specific in each goal as if you were writing an exam question.

Poor Learning Outcome	Better Learning Outcome
Understand Newton's first law	Given two of the three variables in Newton's First Law (F = ma) determine the third variable using appropriate units
Know how to find atomic mass	Given the masses of individual isotopes and their corresponding naturally occurring percentage, calculate the atomic mass of an element.
Describe what each organelle in a cell does	Given a description of a cellular activity, select the organelle that houses that activity

Figure 4.1: Learning Outcomes

Writing Learning Outcomes requires practice. Keep working at it because the clearer you are, the more likely students will know what you expect of them.

Pre-Class Assignments

Students need a reason to look at the modules before coming to class. Your job is to create an assignment that will direct their thinking. So what can you do?

Encourage the students to use the textbook. Simply telling students to read prior to class produces too much cognitive confusion, because most textbooks have far more information in each chapter than a student can effectively process. Asking students to do something with the book as they read requires more cognitive energy than simply reading. Posting a worksheet that students fill out—they could print the worksheet or fill it out interactively on-line—will direct their reading to the content deemed most important by the teacher. If you have the students fill out something for class you could use the assignment as admission to class. Walk around the class and ask students to show you that they've either filled it out or printed whatever you want them to work on that day.

On-line quizzes are one of the most popular means of pre-class work. You could even divide your LOs into pre-class LOs and post-class LOs.

As we will discuss below you could create interactive videos. Use a video from another source (such as Khan Academy) or one that you've created (see next section) and insert questions that students must answer before continuing the video. Even more simply you could include questions about the video in your pre-class quiz.

Pre-Class Videos

Imagine taping yourself for an entire semester then putting those recordings online. Would you have a course worth offering? Clearly not. What is different, though? You still convey the information, you could offer proctored exams, and you could even have office hours. You might think you interact with students a lot in class but most research suggests that you let students talk far less than you think you do. So what exactly is the benefit of a 'live' lecture?

As we'll argue repeatedly throughout this book, you should not be lecturing at all; and that means online as well. When you create a lesson online you need to think in small, manageable chunks. When a colleague asks about how to post a lecture that is two hours long we have realize that the colleague may be asking a technical question but they are really asking a pedagogical one. When you create online videos in the form of screencasts, you need to keep them short. In "Hamlet" Polonius says: "Since brevity is the soul of wit, And tediousness the limbs and outward flourishes, I will be brief." You, too, should be brief because if you talk too much you will become tedious to your students.

Screencasting

A prevalent means of stimulating learning prior to class is screen capture. A variety of programs exist to facilitate screen capture, at the time of this writing the most widely known is Jing, a free software package from TechSmith. Other programs exist such as Camtasia (the full version of Jing), Screenr, and ScreenFlow for PCs and Doceri, ScreenChomp, and DoodleCast Pro for iPads. These programs often have a whiteboard feature that allows inclusion of PowerPoint slides, pictures, and other graphics. We'll examine multimedia design in Chapter 8 and provide a variety of pedagogical rationales for using multimedia resources. For now the focus will be on using screen capture to help your students acquire knowledge. You won't be able to create rich Multimedia design that you see on YouTube channels and you won't be able to create a multimedia platform for your subject the way a company like Rosetta Stone has done for language. You should instead work to make five-minute videos about topics you think they should know about prior to class. KhanAcademy provides good examples although most of those videos are longer than what you want to shoot for.

 "Our life is frittered away by detail. Simplify, simplify (Thoreau, 1854)." Try not to over-explain in your videos. The simpler the better; the shorter the better.

If students find that watching the screen capture presentations proves no more effective in helping them learn than reading the textbook, then the problem with pre-class work has not been solved. Too often, we believe that technology itself will solve the problem as if the problem were words on a printed page. If the words are on a screen with very little audio, then all the teacher has accomplished is a transfer of technology not a change in the pedagogy.

A relatively straightforward use of screen capture is to take existing PowerPoints for a course and narrate them. While opinions differ about the efficacy of PowerPoint, all scholars acknowledge the wide-spread use of the software. As with any popular program, detractors abound. One of the most astute comments we ever heard came from Dave Yearwood, a technology professor at the University of South Dakota. Yearwood said that he wished PowerPoint weren't so easy to use, so not as many people would use it so badly. The ease with which slides can be converted into a movie, however, gives you momentum in designing a blended classroom. Don't fall into the trap of being too simplistic, though. Your goal should be not to merely record what you would normally say in the classroom; your goal is to concisely explain the most challenging points without belaboring those points. Use technology to enhance your out-of-class presentation.

Using audio with the PowerPoint improves the presentation, but only if the PowerPoints are not text heavy. The human mind processes the written word at a different rate than it processes the spoken word. Cognitive dissonance ensues with text-heavy slides accompanied by audio. The use of audio requires some practice: you'll need to learn to modulate your voice appropriately, inject some drama into your presentation. Speak as clearly as possible. Your first few recordings will, most likely, need to be rerecorded, perhaps multiple times.

A more sophisticated approach to screen capture requires the use of storyboarding techniques. The instructor thinks carefully about the message to be conveyed to the student. Just as a film director lays out the scene through the use of images, the instructor creates a story filled with images and with script. The script will serve as the audio portion of the screencast with the images constituting the visual portion. While this type of screencast does take more time the results are generally much more professional. The instructor can add an image or two to lighten the mood, often with an image that might provoke a groan from the viewer. A picture of a dog can be inserted in a discussion of the physiology of digestion with an audio track that explains that the process of digestion starts in the mouth using a different type of "canine." (Groan!) As with teaching itself the type of humor that an instructor shares should align with his or her own personality. An instructor who enjoys groan-inducing puns might include such an image. Ike often draws a cartoon cat on the board with a plus-sign for its belly button and then tell the students that my cartoon represents a 'cat'-ion. Maintaining authenticity in a screencast is the same as maintaining authenticity in the classroom. The learner will know when an instructor is trying to force humor.

 We once attended a workshop titled "Active Learning, Humor, and Rigor: What's the Right Combination?" The implication is that there is competition between humor and rigor. In reality, the answer is easy: use 'em both!

The importance of organizing the screencast ahead of time will pay huge dividends for students who will have to spend less time with material that is effectively presented. A well-placed pun might reengage a student and thus keep the learner more focused. Screencasts should replace portions of your course that used to happen in class. As the content expert you are in the best position to make the type of decisions regarding how best to break down the material into chunks. The chunks of information then require creative multimedia presentations that will help the learner navigate content before ever stepping foot in the classroom.

Student Responsibility

A central concern about a screencast is whether students will watch it before coming to class. You must proceed as if students have completed the screencasts. The issue regarding student completion of work is one of the most often-voiced worries about blended design in our workshops. To alter the pedagogy, the students must not only read the LOs and watch the screencasts but they should have some type of activity to complete. You can create pre-class activities that are automatically graded—either giving a nominal number of points for simply completing the questionnaire, for example, or creating multiple-choice quizzes whose results are automatically entered in a the LMS gradebook—and will therefore save precious grading time. Pre-class quizzes could include a few questions about the screencast. Quizzes are not the only possibility: short writing prompts, creation of a concept map, completing a worksheet. You could decide to assign work prior to class AND give them a quick quiz in class. The goal is to give students a reason for completing all the work you've assigned.

 Accountability should be more carrot and less stick. Give students a few points; use the activity in class if possible; be encouraging about the work by assuming that your students completed the work.

Having students complete the work prior to class creates time for active learning in class. The completion of work during the first few minutes of class can serve as an incentive for the learner to arrive on time and will immediately engage in an activity directly related to the topic for that day. The activity completed at the beginning of class can often catalyze students' questions which will allow you to better craft activities and might lead to changes in the future pre-class screencasts.

Another possibility is to have students complete an activity prior to class and then bring the completed activity to class. The activity could be submitted online and brought to class thus establishing a permanent record on the LMS and prompting students to arrive on time by immediately engaging them in a F2F activity predicated on the completion of the pre-class work. You might want to check the activity as students enter the class, sort of like a passport for entry into the learning environment. If you try such a passport system, be prepared to dismiss students who have not completed the work. A clear message is necessary so that your students will complete the work outside of class.

Students will not be used to such a format the first time so you should have contingency plans prepared for what happens the first time a student doesn't complete the pre-class work. In our workshops we often demonstrate a student-teacher interaction. One of us will gently approach a participant and whisper: "It look like you didn't do the pre-class assignment? You can stay today but you'll have to leave class in the future if you come unprepared. You won't really learn much just by coming to class without adequate preparation." We often contrast such a firm but gentle approach by yelling at another student and stopping the entire class to yell about getting the work done. The contrast is stark.

Assigning work to students prior to class can be humbling for you. We are sometimes challenged by workshop participants who argue that students cannot make sense of the information without expert guidance. In a complex discipline like physics there are genuine fears that screencasts will waste student time and thus complicate the learning process rather than enhancing it. A subject like physics, though, can capitalize on screencasts to introduce a topic to students with a few well-chosen video clips, some engaging visuals, and a brief introduction to the types of problems that will be solved in class.

Preparing for F2F Time

Learning occurs with you and without you. Please pause and reread the last sentence before continuing.

We sometimes feel like therapists when working with instructors, strategically empowering our workshop participants to redesign a course to include blended elements. So here goes: Don't let your lack of experience discourage you. It's natural to struggle, initially, when creating activities for the learner to complete prior to class.

Common excuses for the omission of pre-class materials and work include scientific arrogance ("students cannot learn without me"), poorly-conceived assignments (asking students to read a chapter of a biology text might be akin to asking them to read a chapter of *Anna Karenina* in Russian, because of the number of unknown words), or distrust of students ("they won't do the work anyway, so I'll just wait until I have their undivided attention in class").

To successfully adopt a blended design, examine all your tacit assumptions about learning. Assigning pre-class works requires more introspection on your part than any other aspect of a blended design.

While the concept of asking students to complete work prior to class is not new, the stunning number of ways that technology can engage the learner prior to class is new. Scientific concepts can be explicated in a variety of formats using technology so that students can arrive at the classroom door with some understanding of the content. Low-stakes grading activities ensure that students complete the requisite work. The blended classroom requires creative thinking about pre-class work. Blending will also require your fortitude, because you will be tempted to appease students who will complain they can't understand the pre-class work. You'll be tempted to revert to lecture. Don't give in. You must be strong!

Now that you've designed and successfully integrated pre-class assignments in to your lesson plans and learning objectives, you're be ready to focus on the in-class portion of your blended science course.

CHAPTER 5
IN-CLASS LEARNING: KEEP IT ACTIVE

One of the most common questions we hear about blended courses is what to do during class. When lecture is no longer the primary pedagogy, the usefulness of a teacher in the teacher-centered model seems permanently compromised. Participants in our workshops express concern about being replaced by technology. Such concern stems from a teacher-centric approach: you need to think about what your students are doing not what you are doing.

Pedagogical writers have been arguing for changes in F2F time for decades but faculty have mostly ignored the pleas for change because of the mistaken notion that teaching equals content delivery. While active learning can be accomplished without technology, the pedagogical changes that technology allows can help alter what you students do during class.

Learner-Centered Teaching

The approach we're advocating is learner-centered (Barr and Tagg, 1995b). We want you to think about what your students are doing. We do not want to belabor the point about lecture but if you have not carefully reflected about the learner-centered model of teaching you will find little of substance in this chapter. Why? Because without altering your philosophical approach to learning, any suggestions for actively involving students in the learning process will seem more like entertainment and less like learning.

A learner-centered approach focuses on the mind of the learner. The information in Chapter 1 should help you navigate the choices in a learner-centered approach that capitalize on how your students process information. Class time should be used to engage the learner in activities. If you hold a teacher-centered view, such activities might not seem like learning. Instead of forcing homogeneity us-

Flipped/Blended Lesson Planning Template
Lesson Topic:
Lesson Objectives:
Out-of-Class Activities:
Readiness Assessment:
Flipped Activities:
Assessment:
Resources/Items/ Preparation Needed:

Figure 5.1: Flipped and Blended Lesson Planning Template

ing a lecture, active learning allows students to make sense of the content in unique ways. You won't be a warden in a prison using fear to enforce obedience but instead will be an tour guide who points out many features of the disciplinary landscape with the hope that the learner will start to make sense of the terrain.

Participants in our workshops sometimes challenge the idea of active learning because students often seem like they are having fun: one participant had the temerity to suggest that if students enjoy class time then they are probably not learning! Maybe we'll get more learning as we create more drudgery? We want to ask why, given a choice, would we choose to make learning more difficult? The argument seems to be that life is hard and therefore class should be, too. Any teacher, according to this way of thinking, who finds a way to allow students to enjoy class is failing in their responsibilities to mirror the 'real' world.

 When your student ratings improve, be prepared for criticism that you lack rigor. When students enjoy your class, you may have colleagues who think you have compromised learning.

Being a dull teacher will not work; being a mean teacher will not work. The prefrontal cortex will not allow conscious focus on boring material and the amygdala responds to fear in a protective manner that cuts off thought from reaching the prefrontal cortex. Teachers who rely on fear to try to motivate learning will reduce learning rather than encouraging learning. The goal is to tickle the amygdala enough to arouse it without causing it to overreact in a way that shuts down cognitive processes. And when the neural circuitry is open create ways to keep the prefrontal cortex from being aware that it's engaged in learning.

A learner-centered approach gently coaxes the student to a deeper understanding by trying to approach each learner as an individual capable of such deep learning. Each learner is unique in his or her ability to make meaning of the discipline and the learner-centered teacher will create an environment where the learner feels free to create meaning.

Time

When a teaching approach is geared toward creating activities in which learning can flourish, the teacher's relationship to time alters. In a traditional classroom (where little attention is paid to student learning prior to class and student learning outside of class consists almost entirely of reading, studying, and doing problems) class time is constrained by how much you can cover in a lecture. Ike can remember during his time as an instructor for the Naval Nuclear Power School that colleagues joked about how much we had to cover each day—as you might expect, the lessons were rigidly prescribed—and that if teachers talked faster that would leave enough time for questions. We suggest that you do not talk any faster. You might be tempted to think that talking fast covers more. But the goal is learning and therefore cramming more information into each PowerPoint slide and racing through the slides will actually compromise learning.

Time is not the enemy. When you blend, time becomes more elastic. Instead of worrying about what you will cover that day you might begin wondering what you will have students do that day. On the way to class each day ask: "What are my students going to do today?"

 Have a plan. Create a repertoire of activities that you can choose from during any particular class. Then have confidence in your students to engage in the activity. And, remember, include flexibility in your plan.

Some days students might not seem as motivated. Be attuned to the needs of your learners: be attuned to how they are perceiving time. While you should keep track of time the goal is to help students lose track of time as they focus on an activity. Engaging activities can expand time: there will be days—hopefully many of them—when you'll need to remind your students that another class needs the room. What a wonderful feeling when a class of learners loses track of time so much that they forget they have to leave!

Improvisation is necessary in a learner-centered approach. Your class will be more relaxed without continual time pressure: since you have material available outside of class you won't feel the need to go over everything in class. While a blended design primarily helps the learner, the design will almost surely help you as well. Class time will become more engaging, time will pass more quickly, and you may even have—dare we say it—fun.

Engaging Students/Active Learning

The books available that describe active learning are numerous. One of the best-selling books about student engagement is *Engaging Ideas: The Professor's Guide to Integrating Writing, Critical Thinking, and Active Learning in the Classroom* (Bean, 2011). John Bean is an English professor. You might think that only disciplinary experts can help inform your teaching: chemists read about chemistry teaching, physicists about physics teaching, and so on. So we need to disabuse you of the idea that you can only learn from other experts in your subject area.

Most of the articles you'll read in your disciplinary pedagogy reference authors who are not in your discipline. So you can learn from folks outside your field. In Bean's case one of the most important lessons may be the one on handling the grading load that assignments can create. Bean's first suggestion involves creating a solid assignment. To do so requires careful analysis to determine what you want students to learn from the assignment. You then need to design an effective assignment that you develop into a clear, effective writing (or other type of) project. Bean suggests using rubrics which have been described in the scientific pedagogical literature (Oliver-Hoyo, 2003, Allen and Tanner, 2006).

Another great resource is a book that is now a quarter century old. *Active Learning: Creating Excitement in the Classroom* provides outstanding guidance about how to involve your students in learning (Bonwell and Eison, 1991). Like the suggestions in Bean's book, these ideas are not science-specific but that's okay because neither is learning. Reading pedagogical literature outside your field will help you create activities that are specific to your discipline.

Technology in Class

Much of what is written about pedagogical technology involves work that your students complete either before or after class. There is technological innovation that can improve learning during class. Use clickers to engage students in answering questions. Use a lecture capture program on a tablet and pass the tablet around the class to allow students to teach each other. YouTube videos can help lighten the mood. In the laboratory use computer-interfaces that feed directly into spread sheet programs. If you allow students to bring technology to the classroom (and we sure hope you do) then you open the class to yet another world of opportunities.

As we will detail in later chapters the use of clickers in the classroom can be a simple lever that changes pedagogy completely. Eric Mazur (1997)has written extensively about the use of classroom response systems and Derek Bruff (2009) has a solid collection of suggestions in *Teaching with Classroom Response Systems: Creating Active Learning Environments*. Bruff addresses almost every issue that might arise from clicker use and he does so with the most pedagogically sophisticated reasoning. When asking about how challenging clicker questions should be, for example, he demonstrates clear understanding of neurobiological principles when addressing the rigor of questions.

Keep in mind the role that simpler and easier questions can play in the classroom. A steady stream of challenging clicker questions can mentally exhaust some students. Also, if students consistently answer clicker questions incorrectly, their confidence and motivation can suffer. A few easy questions here and there can give students a break from more difficult questions and bolster their confidence by showing them what they know. Easy questions can also help warm up a group of students at the beginning of a class session for more difficult questions later in the session.

The last point about warming students up is one that seems critically important if an entire class is built on clickers. You want to have a clear idea of the most difficult type of problem that your learner will encounter. Each lesson is then designed backwards. Ask a series of scaffolded questions to gradually generate understanding. If a math problem has multiple parts, the clicker questions should be designed to answer one part at a time, possibly with several questions in a row addressing each component part of the problem. As the class period progresses and students answer the easier questions correctly the difficulty is gradually ratcheted up. The increasing difficulty of the questions throughout a class period mirrors the gaming philosophy of giving an athlete slightly greater challenges.

Writing clicker questions is a skill that will not come easily. The more you write questions and then see the answers that students provide, the better you'll get at writing more questions to excite student learning.

When students bring their own devices (BYOD) into the classroom they can help search for information. We think BYOD makes perfect sense yet if we want to generate hostility in a room of faculty all we need to do is to suggest that they welcome technology into the classroom! Why would so many faculty be threatened by technology? A look at many syllabi will confirm that faculty do not have a love/hate relationship with student technology they have only a hate relationship. The proscriptions against technology are sometimes scathing with faculty threatening to confiscate cell phones, tablets, or laptops. What might be going on?

We have seen that faculty feel threatened by any sort of distraction to the student. In the teacher-centered model students should be paying rapt attention to the words of the teacher. A learner-centered approach recognizes that students learn in different ways and while some students will pay rapt attention others will learn more if they can look something up on a wireless device while the teacher is talking. Some teachers think that students will only use their portable devices for distractions and the use of such a device in class is therefore rude. We recognize the legitimate need to maintain a learning environment that is as free of distractions for other learners as possible but we also think students are experts at surreptitiously using portable devices such that others around them are not even aware that such a device is being used. And if a student takes notes by typing on portable device how is that any more distracting than students scratching pencils against paper? As with many of the issues being discussed in this book, the issue of student technology requires you to take a long, hard look at your own biases. The illusion that all students should politely sit in class and dutifully take notes seems hopelessly outdated. If students are bored then perhaps a reevaluation of your pedagogy is in order. Engaged learners are better learners. The student portable devices are generally not the real issue; the real issue is that teachers do not want to change their pedagogy and resort to authoritarian approach to try to quell an uneasy populace. Fear is again used to try to control the classroom.

The human mind seems to want information. An experiment described in *The Compass of Pleasure* seemed to show that monkeys want information about the future: they want ideas (Linden, 2011).

To my thinking, this experiment is revolutionary. It suggests that something utterly useless and abstract—merely knowing for the sake of knowing—can engage the pleasure/reward circuitry. This is not pleasure obtained from essential things like food or water or sex, which we need to propagate our genes. This experiment suggests that ideas are like addictive drugs.

Learning can be pleasurable—heck, learning should be pleasurable. But our education system seems designed to eliminate any pleasurable feelings. We hope you can find ways to make learning pleasurable.

Synchronizing Your Course

One of the most critically important aspects of a blended design revolves around synchronization: all facets of the design should work together to create a seamless learning environment. Brilliantly designed pre-class movies and activities will enhance learning but brilliantly designed pre-class movies and activities combined with class work that enriches the pre-class learning will create rich pedagogical experiences. The class work should then lead to out-of-class work that helps the learner reflect and rehearse content while also providing opportunities to master the material through work at the higher levels of Bloom's Taxonomy such as analysis, synthesis, and evaluation (Anderson and Krathwohl, 2001, Bloom, 1956).

The challenge of teaching a synchronized course is that each part of the course presents unique challenges and takes significant time to create. You will need to work on specific parts of the course to have the parts mesh as easily as possible.

A Lesson on Evolution

Consider a lesson on evolution. The goal of a synchronous lesson is to ensure that all three phases of learning are being utilized and that class time is usually the central, most active part of the learning process.

- Pre-class: Assign reading via a class guide. Require each student watch a 1-2 short screen capture movies on evolution. Create an on-line quiz that closes prior to class or have students fill out a worksheet covering some of the basics of evolution.

- F2F: As students settle in, hand each group a blank sheet of paper. If you do not have formal base groups established have students count off (kickball strategy as one of my colleagues calls it) into groups of four. One possible assignment is "Rat Island" where students have to imagine an island with a specific ecosystem. Each group is given different parameters and the students must draw a rat that might have evolved in that system.

- After class: Create a quiz that covers more of the information covered in class plus the information from the reading. Or have students do one more project related to rat island where they need to design a different animal using a drawing program.

A Physics Course

Let's look at a physics course where students spend pre-class time watching screen capture movies and then filling out worksheets which they submit via dropbox. The work inside the classroom should then build on the assignment students completed prior to class. Perhaps instead of a drop box students could print the assignment and bring it to class. The instructor could stand at the door and have each student hold up the completed worksheet as they entered the class thus permitting a quick check for completion. During F2F time the activities build on the worksheet—perhaps team work similar to POGIL (process-oriented guided inquiry learning) or clicker questions—to strengthen understanding.

So much of what we normally think of as teaching is accurate only under the teacher-centered approach. Your time is best spent helping each student make sense of the content in our course. Ideally you want a one-to-one tutoring relationship. Active learning approaches this one-to-one model better than any other form of pedagogy. Active learning works best when students have work to do both prior to class that helps prepare them for the learning environment in the classroom. In *Flip Your Classroom: Reach Every Student in Every Class Every Day* the authors point out the benefits of using pre-class work to synchronize with class time (Bergmann and Sams, 2007):

In our combined total of 37 years of teaching, we have been frustrated with students not being able to translate content from our lectures into useful information that would allow them to complete their homework. Then, one day, we had an insight that would change our world. It was one simple observation: "The time when students really need me physically present is when they get stuck and need my individual help. They don't need me there in the room with them to yak at them and give them content; they can receive content on their own."

We have now explored how to create pre-class activities that focus on understanding and comprehension. In this chapter we focused on actively engaging students to help them learn to analyze and apply the pre-class information. Now we need to look at what your students will do after they leave the classroom. We need to examine how to provide activities that help students strengthen what they have learned and to help them think at even higher levels like synthesis and evaluation.

CHAPTER 6
LEARNING AFTER CLASS: INCORPORATING FAILURE INTO YOUR LESSON PLAN

Students shuffle out of your room onto their next class or out into the sunlight of the day. You want them to keep thinking about what you were trying to teach them in class. You want them to consolidate what they've learned. It's not enough to hope that your students will find ways to learn: you can help them.

We know from Chapter 1 that for learning to occur neurons must be restructured and reconnected. Restructuring of neurons requires failure. The need for failure arises from the need to make appropriate connections in the brain. So students need to fail. Once an appropriate connection is made the learner then must reinforce the connection to strengthen the learning, perhaps by confronting challenges that will cause them to fail—at first.

More than any other time in the learning process, the time after F2F instruction affords the optimal opportunities for your learners to reinforce and consolidate knowledge. The human brain forgets most of what it becomes consciously aware of (and it becomes conscious of only a fraction of the input streaming into it) so the most productive way to assist in the formation of long-term memory formation is by repeated exposure (Della Sala, 2010).

The forgetting curve has marked implications in the design of a course. You need to create activities that asks learners to recall information. Every time a student has to recall information the connections in that pathway become strengthened. Consolidation of memories occurs in a variety of ways but two key elements of consolidation are time on task and spacing between the tasks. Your goal is to create activities that encourage time on task and to create spacing between the activities.

We have heard critics of a blended approach say that students need to assume responsibility for their own learning. We are teaching college, they argue, not elementary school. Providing students with resources to direct their learning outside of class is a key element of being a committed educator. One of your roles is to create opportunities for your students to rehearse, and thus consolidate. You want to help make learning as efficient as possible. Unfortunately, you will never quite know when you've done enough to create a learning environment that helps students overcome the forgetting curve. An exciting part of teaching is always working to help every student overcome the forgetting curve.

 Students will forget information if they do not review it. Your job is to create dynamic ways to help them review information.

In the previous two chapters we stressed first exposure prior to class and then active learning in class. Prior to class you create activities that engage your students with the new material: link what is being learned to other courses, activate prior knowledge about the subject, introduce metaphors about the topic, etc. During class we have emphasized active learning. Because students are together with other learners only during class time, F2F time affords unique opportunities. During class collaboration and cooperation play a significant role in the learning process. After class students now need to consolidate. Students may still be actively learning and they may be still constructing new knowledge but the central task after class is to help students solidify the knowledge that they have been exposed to and have actively constructed. Very little—if any—new information should be introduced after class. The goal for after class work should be to help students retain the most pertinent information from pre-class and F2F activities. You need to find ways to keep them from forgetting.

Rehearsal

The easiest way to help buck the forgetting curve is to assign work that requires students to recall previous information. Many times the recall will be faulty. Your students will fail at the act of recall. That's okay!

Deliberate practice is required to learn content so that long-term storage is possible. The effort does not have be drudgery, though. Gamers fail more than 80 percent of the time yet feel good while playing (McGonigal, 2011). Students need to fail in order to learn so they can construct elaborate neural networks. Affording students the opportunity to fail in a low-risk environment will enhance learning. The critical goal after class is to provide activities which allow students to practice and to extend the content in meaningful ways. Practice can take the form of online homework, quizzes, or multimedia interactive activities, all designed to facilitate consolidation.

One means of consolidation is rehearsal. Students need rehearse the information in order to move the information into long-term storage. Students do seem to realize that they need to self-test. A review of self-regulated study found that most students realized that they need to self-test but only a handful (18 percent) viewed self-testing as a learning opportunity (Kornell and Bjork, 2007). Unfortunately, students do not space their studying even though they learn better when they do. In a traditional classroom the teacher often views the idea of telling students how to study as a benefit of F2F instruction but information about how to study can also be conveyed via the LMS. An important consideration in the design of post-class activities is to help your learners become more self-regulated. Sending frequent e-mail reminders with proven study tips can help.

 You need to help students overcome the fluency illusion: they often believe they know more than they do. Ask them questions. They will learn more by questions than by reviewing notes or reading the text.

Self-Testing

One of the best ways to get students to rehearse is through self-testing (Richland et al., 2009). On-line quizzes help students master the content through low-stakes questioning. Weekly quizzes with multiple attempts will ensure that students are at least looking at the material. Creating an online quiz bank for each topic will provide a myriad of ways to help them think about the content. Homework provides practice but a graded quiz usually signals assessment which can serve as self-assessment. Students might not realize that they are rehearsing (and thus learning): when they take each quiz your students will usually be focused on the grade. The focus on grades should not concern the instructor, however, because if the quizzes are well written students will be engaging with the information in meaningful ways. From the instructor's view the points are far less important than the time spent by the learner rehearsing the course content.

Even though quizzes are usually better at stimulating learning, online homework can be helpful. For one thing, homework is a relatively simple means of encouraging time on task. Many text-book publishers have created fairly sophisticated online programs that are intuitive for the user. By assigning a nominal number of points for completion of the homework the instructor signals to the learner that the homework is valued. Teachers should be wary of the system they adopt because in science the input of answers can frustrate students when a rounding error results in the entire problem being marked wrong. Many online homework programs associated with a textbook provided immediate feedback to the learner with hints to help clarify the mistakes that might have occurred. Feedback is becoming more sophisticated.

Many ventures are underway to create more competency-based learning with more inter-activity that guides the student asynchronously through the content. Grading of the homework can be accomplished in multiple ways including: only giving credit for correct answers, giving partial credit, or giving full credit for completing the homework regardless of the number of mistakes. By assigning a nominal number of points the student will receive the message that the work matters to the course grade. Since grades are the coin of the realm, students use graded assignments as a guidepost to determine what the instructor deems important. As with most learner-centered teaching decisions the instructor should carefully reflect on the goal of online homework and then grade in a way that aligns with the teacher's own philosophy and the needs of the learner.

Beyond quizzes and online homework, you can create other ways to encourage your students to think about the information in novel ways. You could require your students to do something like submit three possible test questions in a drop box. You might even use some of their questions on the next exam. You could ask students to do a muddiest point where they submit the concept that they are still having trouble understanding (Angelo and Cross, 1993). A "muddiest point" assignment online can then be used to open the next F2F class or prompt a video that you post covering a topic that was muddy for a number of students. Be creative in finding ways to stimulate learning but keep the number of activities in check. You want to create multiple opportunities to learn but you need to keep the course design manageable so that your students can easily navigate through the course.

Activities at Higher Levels of Cognition

While rehearsal is important for consolidation, after-class time can also be used to extend learning. Rehearsal should be used at least weekly whereas extending knowledge can be done over several weeks. Extension of content can be achieved via term papers, wikis, discussion boards, or student-developed online presentations (iMovies, animations, etc.). The goal is to facilitate deep learning: you want to move students closer to mastery level learning where your learner begins to construct a mental map of the subject.

Developing expertise requires recognizing cognitive guideposts. You want your students to evaluate information and synthesize information. You could assign a primary literature article for them to evaluate, or assign a newspaper or magazine article about a topic and have them evaluate the content. Perhaps a book report on a science popularization is appropriate. In a class on neurobiology, for example, there are a multitude of books written for the general public: assign students to read a book and evaluate it. The same book report could be used to have students synthesize parts of the course into a more coherent whole.

Other projects will have the same general goal: getting your students to work at the highest levels of Bloom's Taxonomy. Creating a wiki page about a topic focuses on both evaluation and synthesis. Creating a movie about a topic will encourage students to synthesize information. Using animation software to convey information to classmates will also facilitate thinking at higher levels of cognition.

Projects that involve technology help students gain technical literacy. While we do not specifically talk about skill development in this book, employers, graduate schools, and professional schools often want students who have a well-developed skill set. Your students will be able to include technical communications on their resume because of the work they do in your course. Written and oral communications can be developed through projects as well as collaborative and leadership skills. Science courses often eschew projects but we encourage you not to ignore the cognitive benefits of projects.

Transparency

We've now traversed the learning cycle: before, during, and after. As your students move through your course, you will want to be as transparent as possible about why you designed the course the way you did. We remind our students regularly about the efficacy of rehearsal. We coax them with the efficiency principle: ten minutes of rehearsal each day for a week will result in more learning than studying 70 minutes straight on the weekend. Students need to hear that reviewing a little each day will result in greater learning gains than doing mammoth study sessions (cramming).

Remind your students about the keys to effective learning and occasionally review the goals of each part of the course. You cannot simply pat yourself on the back for reminding students about rehearsal, however, because strategies for motivating positive behavior are always available. Let's say you are teaching a class where you ask students to review the material prior to the next class, but at the next class it is apparent that the students have not rehearsed. Perhaps it's time to give a short quiz at the beginning of one class and tell students it was a reward for those students who took your advice and reviewed the material: the quiz can be almost identical to a problem that you did in class. You could then tell your students that you will be giving them two more "opportunities" before the next exam to demonstrate that they are taking your advice on learning by reviewing the material each night.

You do not have to be transparent about all aspects of the course. When students take quizzes, they will focus on getting a good grade by retaking the quiz. You don't have to tell them that you are using the quizzes as a formative assessment more than a summative one. It's okay to let the students think that they should try to get every point possible even though in your overall grading scheme quizzes will not count for nearly as much as exams.

Now that you've read about how three parts of your blended course synergize with each other, it's time to look at the technologies that will help you accomplish your learning goals.

Part III
Technology For
Blending

CHAPTER 7
THE TECH ADVANTAGE

The Office of Educational Technology released a sweeping report examining how technology may be used to foster student-centered learning in institutions of higher education in the United States (Brooks, 2016). The report is a supplement to the National Educational Technology Plan released by the office in 2016 that offered a similar vision of educational technology in K-12 schools. Titled "Reimagining the Role of Technology in Higher Education," the report focuses on the challenges and opportunities that colleges and universities face (U.S. Department of Education, 2017).

The document starts with an overview of the "new normal" students currently enrolled in higher education. Drawing on data from the National Center for Education Statistics (NCES), the report identifies that 74 percent of undergraduate students have at least one "nontraditional characteristic." Maybe they have transferred from another institution (66 percent), or work a part-time or full time job (62 percent); some may have a dependent (26 percent) or be a first-generation college student (63 percent). Factor in those students who are attending part-time (43 percent) and those who are enrolled in two-year colleges (35 percent) and you can see that the "nontraditional" umbrella is really inclusive. Recognizing this student population, the report asserts that:

[T]echnology must serve the needs of a diverse group of students seeking access to high-quality postsecondary learning experiences, especially those students from diverse socioeconomic and racial backgrounds, students with disabilities, first-generation students, and working learners at varying life stages— all with differing educational goals, but who all share the desire to obtain a postsecondary credential.

How do we use technology to serve our students needs? Some other recent studies offer some insight. The EDUCAUSE Center for Analysis and Research (ECAR) conducts an annual study on undergraduate students use of technology. Looking across the different annual reports, there is a growing trend in students' appreciation for technology in classroom environments. In the ECAR study released in October 2016, 46 percent of students say they get more actively involved in courses that use technology and 78 percent report that the use of technology contributes to their successful completion of courses (Brooks, 2016). These statistics show a clear student preference for courses that incorporate technology.

Looking specifically at students' views of blended classrooms, the 2016 ECAR study reports that 83 percent of students prefer courses that have some blended components over entirely face-to-face courses (10 percent) or fully online ones (7 percent). Clearly students see advantages to using technology in classrooms. But why? To take a look at some of the advantages that technology can offer, let's meet a few science students. While these are fictional stories, they are based on real students. We've simply changed some names and combined some settings to help the stories demonstrate a few larger concepts.

Emma: Easily Distracted

To begin, let's meet Emma. Emma is a junior enrolled in an upper level biology class. While Emma is really bright and hopes to become a science teacher someday, she also struggles with attention in face-to-face classroom environments. Emma has ADHD and has struggled to focus in lecture-based classes. Emma's biology professor records short lectures and places them online for students to watch prior to coming to class. While these lectures are usually only ten to fifteen minutes in length, Emma reports that it takes her almost an hour to watch some of them. She watches and rewatches some parts so she can fully grasp the concepts being discussed. Emma likes the flexibility that the recorded lessons offer. She can watch them on her smartphone on the bus during her commute or view them on her laptop when she's back at home.

Looking at how technology can support a student like Emma, it's clear that when we make content available online we can make it on-demand for students. They can rewind and re-watch it when needed. This gives students freer access to content and can also play to their strengths. It can help them navigate challenges they may face. For a student with a disability like Emma, the online content gave her ability to watch the lessons free from distractions if she chose.

But there are also advantages for us as instructors. When we record a lesson and place it online, we've created instructional content that can be archived and reused. After several semesters of recording lessons for your blended classes, you'll quickly develop a library of your own videos that you can use across different classes. For concepts that are taught in a variety of courses, a single video can be used multiple times. Marie Norman, co-author of *How Learning Works: Seven Research-Based Principles of Smart Teaching* (Ambrose et al., 2010), offers some advice for "extending the shelf-life of your instructional videos." In an article published in *Faculty Focus*, Marie Norman writes that instructors should avoid references to specific lectures, assignments and assessments and to avoid discussing current events (2017). Avoiding these pitfalls can help you increase the reusability of your recorded videos and save you from having to re-record lessons each semester.

Jamal: College Costs

Let's meet Jamal. Jamal is sophomore enrolled in an introductory chemistry course. While Jamal is studying to become an engineer, this is the only chemistry course he's required to take. Instead of purchasing a textbook that may cost hundreds of dollars for this single class, Jamal is relieved that his professor is using a free chemistry book from OpenStax.

The text is organized similarly to books which Jamal has used for other classes, but he enjoys the interactive nature that the book offers. Rather than just viewing static images in the text, Jamal can click on links to videos and tutorials when he's struggling to understand a concept. The book is viewable on both his iPad and his iPhone so he always has access to his chemistry text wherever he is. Since Jamal is working a part-time job to help pay his way through school, he is able to complete reading assignments when he's on a break from work.

Collegiate textbook prices are growing at a rate three times the Consumer Price Index. In a recent review of Bureau of Labor Statistics data, researchers found that textbook prices have risen over 1000 percent since 1977 (Popken, 2015). Up until the last decade or so, collegiate faculty had few options to relieve the financial burden that students experienced when purchasing textbooks. The emergence of the Open Educational Resource (OER) movement, however, has presented some viable alternatives. OERs are free materials available online that are usually authored individually or collaboratively by experts in a content area. The financial savings from using these "open textbooks" can be significant. One report suggests that "if every student had just one of their traditional textbooks replaced with OER or an open textbook, it would save students in this country more than $1 billion dollars annually (Senack, 2016)."

But the benefits are not just financial ones. Open textbooks allow greater access for students. Students can view open textbooks across a variety of devices and can download them for offline reading. Many OER sites offer inexpensive printing options so students can purchase hard copies if they choose. Open textbooks also allow for revising content if new developments occur. While some scientific content is relatively stable over time, other areas undergo significant change in short amounts of time. These changes force professors to use newer editions and limits students' ability to buy used copies of textbooks. Open textbooks, however, can be easily revised to reflect new developments and discoveries. This revision process allows for greater responsiveness to the changes that happen in some science areas.

Alex: Building Confidence

Let's now meet Alex. Alex is a first year student planning to major in biology. In an introductory physics course required for Alex's program, the professor uses a site called Edpuzzle to embed assessment questions throughout the recorded lessons she places online. Since Alex struggled with physics in high school, he was worried that he'd fall behind and would have difficulty solving complex physics problems at the college level. When the class meets face-to-face, the professor targets her lessons based on what the students missed in the Edpuzzle questions. She then has the students meet in small groups to work on problems and uses clickers to assess whether the students are being successful. Since the professor is constantly assessing the students to see how they're doing, Alex always knows how he's doing and on which areas he still has to work. Solving problems in small groups has also helped Alex gain confidence in his abilities.

Technology offers exciting new assessment opportunities both inside and outside of our classes. With a site like Edpuzzle, you can take a recorded lesson and include questions to keep students engaged and to assess their learning. This assessment data is useful for planning face-to-face instruction and allows you to tailor lessons to the specific areas where students have struggled. This process can also provides tremendous benefits for students as well. Professor Phillip LaRocco, a professor who teaches blended courses at Columbia University, discusses these benefits with his students in an interview online (LaRocco, 2015). One student remarked that the assessments help "you see where you stand in terms of your knowledge."

Looking at the clicker assessments used in Professor LaRocco's class, another student commented that "it's good to have those questions, struggle with them and then get your answers so at the end of the day, even if you struggled, you can leave the class with a clear view." Technology opens the door for us to collect more assessment data from students so we can better direct their learning and help them see where they are developmentally.

Rebecca: Connecting

Let's meet one more student in our discussion on the advantages that technology can offer. Rebecca is a junior studying marine biology. She is completing a research project with one of her upper level biology courses, and has used Twitter to reach out to students and biologists who have done similar research at other colleges. Rebecca's professor modeled this online collaboration by communicating class content and discussions through different social media. For instance, when the class was dissecting different aquatic organisms in lab, the professor asked student groups to use their smartphones to post videos on YouTube and to share photos on Instagram. These media were shared across the class so students could review the dissections conducted by their peers. Rebecca was really excited that a professor from another institution shared her group's video dissection with his students.

Students can learn more than scientific content in our classes. We have the opportunity to teach them broader 21st century skills like collaboration, communication, information literacy and media literacy. Rebecca's story exemplifies some of the possibilities. While sites like Twitter, Instagram and YouTube are often maligned for their misuse or the misinformation they propagate, the sites have instructional upsides. By using social media, students can partner with researchers at other institutions or directly communicate with prominent scientists working in a field of study. As instructors, we can also design lessons that use these sites to broaden the classroom conversations or share media collected from lab environments. In *Talking Science: Language, Learning, and Values*, Jay Lemke observes that,

[s]cience is a social process. This is true even when a scientist is physically alone. Whenever we do science, we take ways of talking, reasoning, observing, analyzing and writing … and use them to construct findings and arguments that become part of science only when they become shared in that community (Lemke, 1990).

Social media offers new avenues for sharing and collaborating with the broader scientific community.

All Students, All the Time

While this chapter has explored only some of the technological advantages for students of science, the array of choices seems dizzying. We'd like to offer you some encouraging advice: not every technology needs to be included into every lesson of every course. You only need a few parts of the technological machinery to make your course hum.

The Tech Advantage

Choose apps, websites and technologies that support student learning. We know that sounds challenging, but our point is that you do not have to become a technophile to utilize technology. When you choose technology, often you are guided by what your institution will support. Keep an eye on how students are using what you provide, and you can learn from students about what other technology might be advantageous.

Diana Laurillard sums it up thusly: [T]echnology offers a range of different ways of engaging learners in the development of knowledge and skills. Precisely because of the richness of possibilities, we have to be careful not to focus simply on what the technology offers, but rather on what the pedagogy requires (Laurillard, 2007).

CHAPTER 8
Multimedia: LEARNING 24/7

If blending is a part of your teaching approach in higher education, the mastery of multimedia needs to be a big lever in your pedagogical toolbox. You should create short videos (called screencasts) that either help introduce a concept or explicate the more difficult aspects of a topic. You can often co-opt other videos and use technology to add question boxes at certain points in the video. The ideas we explore in this chapter involve how to communicate with your students both when you are physically present and when you are not.

At the basic level, learning is accomplished with both the spoken word and various forms of visuals (text, pictures, animations etc.) The learner attends to aspects of the presentation, holds it in their working memory then integrates the organized pieces into any relevant prior knowledge. Too often teachers violate this simple principle by reading text directly from a PowerPoint slide. Multimedia involves more than just PowerPoint, though. You could be using a White Board the way many Khan Academy videos do or narrating a picture that you have on screen.

As we mentioned in Chapter 1, from a neurobiological standpoint, instructors need to be keenly aware that we can easily overwhelm students' working memories. In figure 1, consider working memory as a desktop where students need to keep a number of items within easy reach. Items refer to all forms of information, facts, symbols, diagrams, words and pronunciation which together constitute cognitive load. Too much cognitive load can interfere with learning if we exceed the learner's working memory. Mayer's diagram is worth exploring in detail because he has done significant research trying to understand how multimedia should be designed to maximize learning (Mayer, 2009).

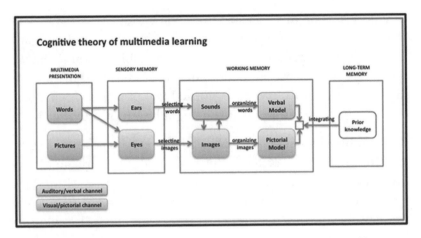

Figure 8.1: Conceptualization of multimedia learning theory adapted from Mayer

The presentation is represented by the left-most rectangle. Mayer uses the dual coding assumption, i.e. the learner attends to information through eyes and ears. Each coding stream is trying to filter out noise and to make sense of what is being presented. Note that words are processed by eyes and ears whereas as pictures are only processed through the eyes. Extraneous words will cause distraction in sensory memory. The working memory rectangle uses the limited capacity assumption, i.e. learners have a finite amount of working memory capacity and it can be overloaded. Students often overload themselves by trying to multi-task but you can unwittingly cause overload via poor design. The final rectangle represents the active process of integration. The consolidation of memory can only occur when students actively engage with their visual and auditory channels.

Mayer's work has identified 12 important principles which deal with three assumptions: dual processing of information, limited working memory capacity, and active integration of images and words. The principles should help guide you in creating screencasts as well as during your in class explanations.

1. **Coherence Principle** – People learn better when extraneous words, pictures and sounds are excluded rather than included. Less is more when it comes to learning. As an academic you may have

trouble accepting this principle since you will almost always know more than the learner. While you don't want to dilute the disciplinary message you want to be as concise as possible. If you add fancy transitions, moving backgrounds, and complicated image that are not directly relevant then you have violated this principle. Powerpoint has a plethora of features that you might be tempted to use: don't!

2. **Signaling Principle** – People learn better when cues that highlight the organization of the essential material are added. Now PowerPoint features might be put to better pedagogical use. Introduce one item at a time on a slide to gradually build toward a complete meaning. Use arrows to direct the learner's attention. Use colors to highlight important works. Tim has done research on eye tracking in anatomical sciences, a visually complicated environment with an accompanying language required for comprehension. He has found that simply by showing students where to look with a single dot, they do significantly better than those student who were not given the dot for attention. Furthermore, the people who got the dot early seemed to learn how to figure out the salient parts of the visuals and continued to do better even when the guidance was removed (Roach et al., 2016, Roach et al., 2017).

3. **Redundancy Principle** – People learn better from graphics and narration than from graphics, narration and on-screen text. This principle has an odd name: it doesn't mean repeat yourself all the time. What the principle does suggest is that you not duplicate information. Don't write words on slides other than for signaling. You speak to the slide in a story-like fashion using the keywords but not reading them directly.

4. **Spatial Contiguity Principle** – People learn better when corresponding words and pictures are presented near rather than far from each other on the page or screen. Remember older maps from yesteryear, perhaps the pull down maps at the front of the sixth grade classroom? Sometimes these maps had letters and numbers in the countries which related to a legend way down at the bottom of the map telling us the population of this country, the natural resources of that region, or the geological characteristics. This principle tells you *not* to use these types of maps. The closer you put your signal-

ing words to the part of the image that you are trying to signal, the clearer your message will be.

5. **Temporal Contiguity Principle** – People learn better when corresponding words and pictures are presented simultaneously rather than successively. Temporal contiguity relates to the time at which signals are presented. Don't explain a picture in detail before you show the picture. Doing so creates excessive load on the learner's brain as he or she tries to create meaning and construct mental schema. We often find that new professors are a bit too passionate about their subject and forget that their learners don't have their depth of knowledge. Simple is better, signaling is better, and contiguous is better

6. **Segmenting Principle** – People learn better when a multimedia lesson is presented in user-paced segments rather than as a continuous unit. When you create a screencast for your class keep them short and allow students to pause throughout. Mayer found that having designated 'pause' points where the student might self-assess before continuing helps improve learning outcomes.

7. **Pre-training Principle** – People learn better from a multimedia lesson when they know the names and characteristics of the main concepts. This concept aligns with the idea that students can do a lot to prepare for class. Before students watch a video they should have read over the Learning Outcomes so that they are aware of the projected outcomes for a topic. A list of words, a few key ideas, or a few simple explanations can help prepare the learner for the multimedia.

8. **Modality Principle** – People learn better from graphics and narrations than from animation and on-screen text. This principle is similar to #3 and essentially says that words at the bottom of the screen explaining a concept do not work as well as the spoken word.

9. **Multimedia Principle** – People learn better from words and pictures than from words alone. This principle seems obvious yet college teachers often think that words are enough. Teachers can overexplain concepts to the point that they may start to sound like Charlie Brown's teacher to the student: "wah-wah-wah-wah…."

10. **Personalization Principle** – People learn better from multimedia lessons when words are in conversational style rather than formal style. All three authors subscribe whole-heartedly to this principle but that can sometimes put as at odds with colleagues. We want conversational rapport with students, not formal diction. When you narrate a video try to let your personality shine through. Your personality allows students to better associate the learning with a friendly voice and voices are important as the next principle demonstrates.

11. **Voice Principle** – People learn better when the narration in multimedia lessons is spoken in a friendly human voice rather than a machine voice. Think about whether you would rather hear a machine when you call a doctor's office or hear a person. Your students still want to hear you.

12. **Image Principle** – People do not necessarily learn better from a multimedia lesson when the speaker's image is added to the screen. This principle is humbling: students want to hear you but they do not need to see you. Your image does not necessarily distract them because the learning seems to be the same either way. So if you want to be seen then include a picture but otherwise—if you're like us—you'll be happy to leave your picture off the screen.

 These twelve principles may seem self-evident but they are all backed by solid evidence. You might sometimes violate the principle without realizing it so we suggest recording a screencast and then going through Mayer's principles to ensure that you are not saddling your learner with extraneous information.

CHAPTER 9
COLLABORATIVE LEARNING: STUDENTS HELPING STUDENTS

Collaboration has been identified as a critical skill for individuals to "survive and thrive in a complex and connected world (Trilling et al., 2009)." Describing the 21st century workplace, the same report notes that "today's knowledge work is done collaboratively in teams, with team members often spread across multiple locations, using a digital zoo of devices and services to coordinate their project work."

Lawrence Summers, a former Harvard president, argues that collaboration is the "inevitable consequence of the knowledge explosion (Summers, 2012)." The world is becoming a more open place, Summers writes, and businesses are placing a greater value on the ability to work together.

With the world becoming increasingly connected and people working and learning from a distance, collaboration needs to be a curricular focus in your courses and cultivated in your classrooms. We just can't expect students to know how to collaborate. It's a skill that needs to be developed. But cultivating collaboration isn't easy, especially in educational settings.

Like so many concepts, collaboration skills are best learned socially and contextually. Students learn to collaborate by directly communicating and working with their classmates—either in the classroom or virtually. As a teacher you can support collaboration and you can help students learn from collaborative experiences through better design.

Is collaboration happening in our classrooms? Summers doesn't seem to think so. Examining the current state of America's institutions of learning, Summers writes, "the great preponderance of work a student does is done alone at every level in the educational system... For most people, school is the last time (students) will be evaluated on individual effort."

Collaborative Technologies

In this chapter, we'll explore collaborative technologies for the blended science classroom. These tools will broaden communication opportunities, and others can make the face-to-face portion of a blended science course more engaging..

Wikis

Most people know about wikis (http://www.wiki.com/) only from their use of the online encyclopedia, Wikipedia. But Wikipedia is actually just one example of a wiki. Wikis are webpages that can have multiple authors and editors. While a wiki can be set for public or private viewing, its utility and benefit arise from the collaboratively-generated content.

Imagine you're teaching the history of atomic theory in an introductory chemistry class, rather than just have the students read a chapter in the book or watch a video lecture on the topic, you can create collaborative teams that research the different atomic models or scientists throughout time. Each team can be given different pages within a wiki where they share their research with the other members of the class.

In a way, wikis function like a technological potluck dinner. The entire "meal" results from the digital entrees, side dishes, and desserts that each team contributes. The whole wiki develops from the research that each team adds to the space. While some people worry that the task of editing a wiki can lead to misinformation being shared among groups, the process can actually help to build critical information literacy skills and offer lessons in vetting information.

If you're just starting out with wikis, wikispaces (www.wiki-spaces.com) is an easy-to-use wiki designed especially for educators.

The Google Suite

Google offers a suite of online collaborative tools that can support students enrolled in a blended course. Google Docs provides collaborative word processing capability that can be useful in supporting students who are completing a group writing assignment. Google Slides supports the construction of group presentations and Google Sheets can aid with group data collection and analysis. While the Google tools offer a great deal of possibilities, it is important to remember the quote from Diana Laurillad that we shared at the end of Chapter 7. We can't just focus on what any individual technology offers. Instead, we should focus on what the pedagogy requires.

Blogs

Blogs are online journals that students can use to capture their development and their thought process. A source about blog use in college concluded that: "Blogs are useful teaching and learning tools because they provide a space for students to reflect and publish their thoughts and understandings. And because blogs can be commented on, they provide opportunities for feedback and potential scaffolding of new ideas. Blogs also feature hyperlinks, which help students begin to understand the relational and contextual basis of knowledge, knowledge construction and meaning making" (Ferdig and Sweetser, 2004).Here is a list of the most common blogging platforms:

- WordPress.org
- Wix
- WordPress.com
- Blogger
- Tumblr
- Squarespace
- Joomla
- Ghost
- Weebly

When students write and comment on each other's blogs, this supports collaborative learning. Such collaborative understanding can be important in science, especially when tackling difficult concepts. Part of the utility of blogs in science classes is that "[the] posting and comment cycle helped clarify and explain posts, as well as challenged ideas and began discussion (Brownstein and Klein, 2006)." Besides having students individually write blogs, research teams can use blogs to journal about their work and document and reflect on their findings. While a variety of blogging platforms exist, Wordpress (www.wordpress.com) offers a large degree of flexibility for you and your students.

Twitter

Twitter is a social networking tool that can be a powerful addition to the blended science classroom. As your students interact with instructional content before coming to class, Twitter can provide a collaborative environment for them to interact with one another and with you. Although Twitter has a unique lexicon and norms of practice that may be a little intimidating at first, posting and responding through the system is easy. Twitter uses a "hashtag" system to make posts (called "tweets") easy to find. Instructors can create a hashtag for their class (#CHEM101, for example) that students can use when they tweet. Used as part of a blended classroom cycle, students could tweet a question they have after watching a recorded lecture. A student could tweet something like:

Calculating at wt of H20 & still coming up short #help #CHEM101

which would alert you that you may need to spend some time reviewing the atomic weight calculation when the class meets during class.

Classroom Games

We thought we'd finish with something fun. While some of our colleagues balk at the notion that collegiate classrooms can be fun and engaging spaces, we do not. We believe that collegiate science classrooms can be more entertaining and engaging without reducing the intellectual and instructional elements of the course. Several technologies allow you to assess students as they compete individually or as a team to answer questions. Use tools like Kahoot (getkahoot.com), Socrative (socrative.com) or Quizalize (www.quizalize.com).Each of these allow instructors to add content-based questions that students can access with a laptop, smartphone or tablet.

If integrating games in your course sounds complicated, it's not. For instance, let's say you've assigned students to watch a video lecture prior to class and want to assess how many students understood the concepts presented in the lesson. By adding some multiple choice, knowledge-based questions in Kahoot, you can start the face-to-face class with a team assessment.

As we've written, assessing students as they progress through the learning stages is crucial. With classroom games, you'll be able to assess student learning, but do it in a collaborative and engaging way. Collaboration often seems as though it slows down the learning process. After all, when students talk to each other their thoughts are often messy and uninformed. However, the beauty of a blended course is that you create time to allow collaboration and in doing so improve student success and satisfaction. After all, shouldn't you *and* your students enjoy the course?

CHAPTER 10
F2F TECHNOLOGY: MAKING IT CLICK

In Teaching Naked: How Moving Technology Out of Your College Classroom Will Improve Student Learning, the argument is made that a blended design should keep technology outside the classroom walls (Bowen, 2012). The "naked" interaction between instructor and learner takes precedence. The dynamic between instructor and student can be powerful and the interaction between these two parties must be carefully considered in the pedagogical design process. But the naked interaction, the interaction sans technology, is only a tool in the same way that technology is a tool.

Because the classroom space is important, careful planning for face-to-face interactions is necessary. When you design a class the goal should not be how to create more naked interactions. To think so narrowly about the importance of the classroom unwittingly reinforces the instructor-centered paradigm. The goal of education is to alter the mind of the learner in substantive and meaningful ways. You should deploy as many resources as possible toward this goal. Perhaps you should consider moving more technology into your classroom in order to interact with your students.

Integrating Technology

Classroom Response System
One of the most important pieces of F2F technology is the classroom response system, often called a clicker. Early in the spread of this technology, students needed clicker hardware but now they can use a cell phone if the appropriate software is employed or use a text-based system like PollAnywhere. Regardless of how the students input their answers, the technology for clickers makes students active, real-time participants in the learning process.

Eric Mazur is considered the exemplar for clicker use in science courses and his design. Clickers can improve the dynamic of your science class: "Experience shows that the use of clickers transforms the classroom, mostly in positive ways (Duncan, 2005)." The motivational aspects of using clickers augments the active nature of the classroom. Students cannot sit passively assuming that they understand a concept; they must actively participate.

The most important aspect of clickers seems to be that students must commit to an answer. Students who simply watch an instructor solve a problem can convince themselves in hindsight that they knew the answer all along. This is called the fluency illusion—a concept nicely explained in *How We Learn* (Carey, 2014). Students who use a clicker must select an answer and when that answer proves incorrect they have less psychological motivation to equivocate concerning their understanding of a topic. By keying in an incorrect answer the student is less likely to succumb to the fluency illusion.

Clickers create a learning environment where failure can be tolerated. By accepting mistakes your students can then start the difficult work of clarifying their thinking rather than equivocating about whether they really knew the right answer. From a student's perspective alone, the ability to test their understanding through anonymity is a great advantage for two reasons. First, the social pressures of "getting stuff wrong" is eliminated with many clicker activities unless the student wishes to share their results. Secondly, the ability to give "just in time" feedback aligns with the "Seven principles for good practice in undergraduate education," one of which is the importance of timely feedback (Chickering and Gamson, 1987).

The most common use of clickers is for multiple-choice questions in large-enrollment courses were student engagement might otherwise seem difficult to achieve (Duncan, 2005, Crouch and Mazur, 2001, Mazur, 1997). Using clickers only for multiple-choice questions does not fully capitalize on the pedagogical potential that clickers offer. Clickers can improve student outcomes, a finding reported in two meta-analyses (Hunsu et al., 2016, Chien et al., 2016).

A robust study lead by Mayer found that using clickers increased student grades by one-third of a grade point (Mayer et al., 2009). As students accept clickers you can look for creative ways to use them to facilitate learning and invigorate your own pedagogy.

A seemingly obvious goal of using clickers is to have the entire class give the correct response to a given question. The route to student success, however, is to ask questions that are slightly more challenging than students are ready to answer. One key to Mazur's (1997) strategy is to prompt peer conversation. The act of conversing with a classmate, articulating reasons for a particular answer is more important than getting the correct answer: the process of getting to the answer is as important as the answer itself. Understanding how to think about a problem, or learning in general, is called metacognition. A study on clickers suggested that metacognition from clicker use is more a more productive influence on the learning process than in the control group that did not use clickers (Brady et al., 2013).

When writing clicker questions you should think about how to gradually increase the difficulty of the questions you ask. This scaffolding process will allow students to become confident with the simpler concepts and will then use the clicker questions to 'climb' to higher levels of understanding.

Lecture Capture

Another way to involve students in class is with a tablet that you can pass around the room so that students can write on the tablet while the images are projected on the screen. The use of a tablet has been advocated as an effective lecture component (Rogers and Cox, 2008), but your goal should be student inter-activity. Project the tablet onto the screen in the classroom and ask students to work through a problem or a reaction mechanism or draw a cell. Students can write on the tablet and the program captures the image. Audio can also be recorded to produce a short movie that students can then view outside of class.

As we argue throughout this book lecture should be minimized whenever possible. A lecture capture might not alter the pedagogy but the capture provides one more tool for students to use outside of normal class time. The ideal use of lecture capture seems to be finding ways to involve the students in the creation of mini-modules that can be posted on the course LMS. Technology in the form of lecture capture can help empower the learner by providing opportunities to rehearse inside and outside of class.

PowerPoint

Creative ways of using PowerPoint are now available. Simply using more animation in PowerPoint, having images appear one at a time can help students focus on one concept before proceeding to another. You could create a large single PowerPoint slide, similar to the format often used to generate research posters to provide space for writing. You can create the slide outside of class and then post the slide for students or use F2F time to collectively generate the slide during class.

One of the benefits of having a large slide is that "students will zoom in and out of the [metabolic] maps and use the hand tool to scroll around the integrated maps." Concept mapping can be combined with PowerPoint to help encourage students to link concepts in the same way that a large metabolic map might do. There is free software available—such as Prezi—where a large poster-sized slide can be viewed as an overview and then more directly by zooming into particular areas for concentration.

This approach is useful to generate a concept map from class. The big picture ideas are held in place while you can "bore down" by zooming into a particular subset of equations, metabolic pathways, or underlying anatomy, for example. Since the software is freely available and web-based, it also a potentially strong tool for student collaborations and presentations.

Digital Pens

Digital pens such as Livescribe are becoming more prominent. Instructors can capture their entire lecture using a digital pen or use the pen for shorter segments and post those segments. The use of shorter segments allows for easier labeling and provides students with more organization. The shorter the segments, the more likely that students will use them. Individual oral exams could be given using a digital pen so that the instructor has a copy of both the student's writing and audio. Students might also choose to use a pen to take notes which would help the learner take more control.

Videos

This is universally-accepted among higher education researchers: visual aids improve student learning. The number of videos amassed on YouTube is staggering (more than a billion at last count with 300 hours of new video posted every minute). Because teaching will never be perfect, a teacher can be consoled with videos that are good enough. You can learn to improve your search queries to find more relevant videos but you can also enlist students for help: student presentations often utilize a video that augments the presentation.

A valid question is whether to use videos in-class or assign them for students to watch on their own time. Use learning goals to guide you. Short videos ratchet up the excitement during class. A short clip can serve as a springboard for discussion or can lighten the mood with a funny application of a concept.

Watching longer videos during class may be difficult to justify because of the passive nature of the video. A twenty-minute TED talk might be important enough to spend class time watching, but when you encourage students to watch assigned videos prior to class, more time is available for active learning. As you may well suspect, students are a crafty bunch and if they feel that the video is too long, or the message is mixed, they will begin to watch it at 1.5-2x speed.

If you use a piece of media such as a video for pre-work prior to your face-to-face encounters, be prepared to discuss it with the class and possibly have a low-stakes pre-class quiz to reward students for good pre-class preparation. Remember that if your lectures are simply "captured" and represent the only method of interacting with the instructor, students will treat those materials as tool for cramming prior to exams. Cramming leads to little long-term learning or meta-cognitive activity.

Lab Hardware & Software

Of all the places within the science curriculum where technology is used, the laboratory is probably the place where the most technologically advanced hardware is integrated: pH meters, NMR spectrometers, oscilloscopes, IR spectrophotometer, UV-Vis spectrophotometers, mass spectrometers, PCR machines, microscopes, and DNA sequencers, to name a few. A recent article on laboratory technology clearly summarized the benefits: "Data acquisition systems are an extremely useful form of educational technology that can be used alone or in conjunction with other technologies to bring about active learning and enable students to move beyond memorization to the verification strategies and knowledge base they need to successfully master chemistry concepts (Milner-Bolotin, 2012)."

Laboratory learning in science education should receive more pedagogical scrutiny. When faculty are surveyed, goals such as developing laboratory techniques and critical thinking are cited (Bruck et al., 2010, Bretz et al., 2013). Journals routinely publish laboratory experiments, but those experiments are almost always about *how* to conduct the lab not *why*, at least not why in the pedagogical sense. Often the "why" behind laboratory learning is treated as self-evident.

Consider this sentence from the summary of a detailed description of an otherwise pedagogically sound laboratory experiment: "This experiment helps to *expose* students, relatively new to the field of biochemistry, to the myriad possibilities of sugar chemistry (Herdman et al., 2012)." Consider this lab summary: "This lab exercise is a great way to *present* the invertebrate phyla in a few hours (Davis-Berg, 2011)." Laboratory learning is often designed to "expose" and "present" rather than "involve." Involvement seems like a given probably because students are assumed to be actively engaged in the laboratory. Your job is to make sure that students are involved.

According to a 2014 article published in *Current Biology*, "experimental records that aren't being digitized account for 17 percent loss of all research data and lab books are becoming the bottlenecks in information management. This poses great repeatability threats, enormous costs and considerable limitations for knowledge sharing within an organization and the community."

Using data acquisition software such means that students no longer have to write data in a notebook or type the data into a spreadsheet. Software packages for laboratories seem to always be appearing. The goal for laboratories is to think about how technology can augment the student experience, instill the skills, animate the principles at hand, and give students another layer of experiential learning.

Here is a list of some of the best digital notebook software programs available for your students to use:

1. Scinote

2. Benchling

3. Rspace

4. DoColLab

5. LabFolder

6. LabArchives

Student Technology

Here's a story about keeping technology in the classroom. An instructor was teaching a communications course and wanted to engage students in a debate about publicly accessible information. One student raised his hand and asked if University salaries at public institutions were a matter of public record. The instructor said that they were but the debate was how easily accessible those records should be made. Less than 10 minutes later the same student raised his hand and said that accessing information is already pretty easy. As an example the student asked the instructor if he would like to know who the lowest paid member of the communications faculty was at that particular state institution. The instructor smiled wanly, complimented the student on his diligence, and then said that he probably did not want to know the answer to the student's question. The student smiled and assured the instructor that it was probably better that he didn't know.

When we do workshops we are routinely shocked by how adamant faculty can become about the importance of students not using any technology in the classroom. We attribute this stance to a worrisome underlying cause: faculty do not trust students. The goal of shutting down technology seems to be that students would use the technology inappropriately. When we suggest that the role of the teacher should be to create such a stimulating learning environment that students will want to pay attention we are often greeted with incredulous looks. The communication instructor found that at least one student in his class was using technology to augment, not hinder, learning. Many teachers seem to place prohibitions on technology because they believe that the technology is the issue. The issue, though, is the pedagogy not the technology.

When the classroom or laboratory becomes a dynamic learning environment then technology can become a useful and complementary tool. Clicker questions can now be answered using cell phones. How exciting for students to be told to make sure all their phones are turned on! When students have technology turned on, they can continually fact-check the instructor or group mates. We always should want students to check our facts, look for additional information, or generate questions. Technology will become a larger part of your F2F classroom experience. Embrace it!

CHAPTER 11
STUDENT SELF-ASSESSMENT

At a blended workshop we conducted, one of the attendees asked us to help her revise a blended lesson she had used in one of her biology classes. She explained that she had recorded several lectures and that students had watched the videos prior to coming to class. During class, she planned active learning activities. Several days later, she gave her students a quiz on the material and was surprised to see many of the students had done poorly. She said that many of the students had found the video lessons to be educational and had anticipated doing well on the quiz. "Maybe," she said, "blending doesn't work in biology classes."

When instructors start using blended learning, they often focus on providing instructional content for students and incorporating activities for students. While these processes are critical to blended success, focusing too heavily on these areas misses the most important aspect of blended learning success: assessment. Put simply, **assessment** is the fuel that drives the blended learning engine. To be successful, assessment opportunities need to be thoughtfully incorporated into each phase and used to inform subsequent phases.

Let's return to our biology colleague. While she had planned for presenting content to her students and building engaging activities to use during class, she didn't build distinct assessment opportunities into the different phases of her blended lessons. She incorporated a quiz at the end of the cycle to assess what the students had learned overall, but she had missed critical opportunities to learn *from* her students along the way. That's what makes assessment the critical driver in the blended cycle.

Faculty naturally associate the term "assessment" with quizzes and exams. These tools are referred to as **formal assessments**, and are usually high-stakes assessments. In reality, these high-stakes activities represent a small subset of assessment opportunities.

Assessments may be broken into two larger categories: **summative and formative**. Most of our experience with assessment comes in the form of summative assessment. For example, we have our students take exams or write papers. Summative assessments are valuable because they let us know whether our students have successfully learned what we wanted them to learn. However, because summative assessments usually serve at some endpoint of instruction, they provide little information to guide teaching along the way.

Blended learning courses must incorporate what are called **formative assessments** to avoid the pitfall in which our biology colleague found herself. As summative assessments are assessments **"of"** learning, formative assessments are assessments **"for"** learning. They help guide instruction and provide valuable information for the instructor *and* for the learner. Formative assessments drive instructional decision-making and allow the instructor to "take the temperature" of the class.

The biology instructor had planned a summative assessment at the end of the unit, but had not incorporated any opportunities for formative assessments along the way. She didn't know the gaps in her students' learning until the end of the instruction— when it was too late.

Let's examine the assessment opportunities in the blended cycle and discuss ways that formative assessment can be incorporated to "take the temperature" of a class and inform the instruction along the way.

Before Class—Formative Assessment

In the beginning phases of the blended learning cycle, students interact with content before coming to class. While students may be working on their own away from our classrooms, there are still assessment opportunities for us as instructors. For instance, we can use tools like Edpuzzle (www.edpuzzle.com) or PlayPosit (www.playposit.com) to embed questions in a recorded lecture. These embedded questions assess students as they watch the video and determine if they're mastering the important concepts being taught. In addition to embedding questions in a recorded lecture, you can create a short quiz that can be administered through the Learning Management System. Similarly, you can require students complete a problem set as a "ticket in the door" to gain admittance to the face-to-face lesson.

While all of these assessments may sound like a lot of work to manage, these assessments don't necessarily have to be graded assignments. Incorporating "low stakes" assessment motivates students to learn the material and will let you (and your students) know where they are in their mastery of the class materials and concepts. Before-class formative assessments will shape and inform your in-class instruction and help you target students' gaps in learning.

During Class—More Formative Assessment

In chapter 10, we talked up clickers. As students complete clicker questions, you can monitor student learning to identify concepts and terms that may need further attention and instruction. As you may have already guessed, the technology tools outlined in chapter 10 may be used as formative assessments. Likewise, the collaborative tools discussed in Chapter 9 offer opportunities to assess students at a low-stakes level.

You should also be prepared to leverage active learning tools and strategies as assessments. To be effective, active learning strategies involve every student. In a lecture class, you may call on a single student to gauge the depth of learning among the students. If you've read this far, you know that this is a terrible way to gauge student learning and not the kind of assessment you should use in a blended course. Instead, use a Muddiest Point activity. Students complete a quick writing assignment in which they explain what was the muddiest point from a lesson (Angelo and Cross, 1993). Collect the Muddiest Point papers as "tickets out the door," then use the data you collect to plan after-class activities.

After Class—Summative Assessment

As you reach the after-class phase in the blended learning cycle, you will start to employ summative assessments, especially if you've reached the end of a unit. Ideally, these summative assessments such as quizzes, exams, portfolios and papers are scheduled after students have received feedback on formative assessments they have completed. Additionally, summative assessments should be seen as opportunities for students to integrate what they've learned from across lessons and activities.

To prepare for these summative assessments, students can be recruited to develop assessment questions for their peers. A tool such as PeerWise (peerwise.cs.auckland.ac.nz) may be used to challenge students to author their own assessment questions and help them focus on the important concepts and learning outcomes of a course. Developing effective alternatives encourages students to reflect on possible misconceptions. Explaining an answer to a question in their own words reinforces student understanding.

The Dunning-Kruger Effect

Returning to our biology colleague from the start of this chapter, there's another assessment lesson to take away from her story. She explained that the students had anticipated doing well on her quiz when she asked them. New learners often fall prey to something called the Dunning-Kruger effect and overstate their own abilities. Since undergraduate students are often new to our content areas, the Dunning-Kruger effect tells us we shouldn't rely heavily on our students' self-reported assessments of their learning. Asking questions such as, "Does anyone have any questions?" or "Do you feel like you understand this?" won't give reliable data on students' knowledge gaps.

The Dunning-Kruger effect was first introduced in 1999. Students' abilities to self-evaluate their performance was studied and evaluated. After taking a test on logical reasoning, grammar or humor, participants were asked to assess their overall test score and to rate their performance against those of their peers. Across the study, students who performed in the bottom quartile of the survey group consistently perceived their test score and performance relative to their peers as far greater than they actually performed. As the study's authors pointed out, "participants in general overestimated their ability with those in the bottom quartile demonstrating the greatest miscalibration (Kruger and Dunning, 1999)."

To relatively new faculty, the Dunning-Kruger effect may be eye-opening. If you've been teaching for some time, however, you probably recognize this phenomenon in practice. Charles Darwin recognized the Dunning-Kruger effect in *The Descent of Man* where he writes, "ignorance more frequently begets confidence than does knowledge (Darwin, 1874)."

Students aren't always aware of what they don't know. That's why using formative assessments and providing frequent and ongoing feedback is so important. In the Kruger and Dunning study, the researchers point out that the negative feedback from grades offers little support for participants' growth. Kruger and Dunning write, "Although our analysis suggests that incompetent individuals are unable to spot their poor performances themselves, one would have thought negative feedback would have been inevitable at some point in their academic career (Kruger and Dunning, 1999)."

Successful educators help students develop the meta-cognitive abilities to successfully self-assess their knowledge base and performance. As novices in our content areas, students will not have the ability to readily identify what they know from what they don't know. By offering ongoing formative assessment during all phases of the blended learning cycle, we can provide developmental markers to help guide students and have them overcome the gaps in their learning. While the Dunning and Kruger research identifies individuals as "ignorant" or "incompetent," we prefer to view students as "learners" to whom we provide the necessary feedback and supports to help them be successful in our blended science classrooms.

This chapter was contributed by Happy Gingras and Patricia Adams from their book, *Blended Learning and Flipped Classrooms: A Comprehensive Guide*, Part-Time Press (2017).

CHAPTER 12
MEASURING INSTRUCTOR SUCCESS

Measuring The Success of Your Class

All too often, the success of a class, student and instructor are simply measured by the grades that the students have earned in the class. However, there are other kinds of information and data that need to be considered when measuring the success of a class: student engagement, student retention and instructor satisfaction also need to be considered.

Students who are engaged with the course materials stay in the class. "Student engagement in educationally purposeful activities during the first year of college had a positive, statistically significant effect on persistence, even after controlling for background characteristics, other college experiences during the first college year, academic achievement, and financial aid" (Kuh, Cruce, Shoup, Kinzie and Gonyea, 2008). Students who are engaged with course content learn the course content. These outcomes are strongly correlated with an active classroom. The flipped and blended course sets students up for success since flipping and blending allow for engaged, active learning.

Instructor satisfaction is another key in determining the success of your class. "Faculty are the linchpins to student success. They are at the center of student success not just as individual pieceworkers in increasingly large classrooms, but as a collective, engaged in various departmental and organizational initiatives to enhance student achievement" (Rhodes, 2012). Faculty matter in facilitating student engagement and success (Umbach and Wawrzynsky, 2005).

Instructors who create active learning course content will be more engaged with the course material. Why? The blended classroom moves beyond the hour-long "sage on the stage" lecture format and morphs it into a dynamic, challenging environment where course materials are created and analyzed (higher-level thinking goes on). The instructor is engaged, working alongside the students, creating and analyzing.

Final Grades

Do not get us wrong, summative [high-stakes] assessments are an important measure of student success. Grades are the measure by which students are expected to be judged. However, remember that final student grades as a measure of student success (and your success as an instructor) may not be perfect. We recommend including the students' final grades as part of your determination of how successful your class was, but not to rely solely on that measurement.

 It's important to remember that you will have students who come to class prepared, ask excellent questions and engage you in conversations outside of the classroom. Such students may nonetheless do poorly on tests. Twenty percent of college students report suffering from test anxiety (American Test Anxiety Association, 2013). Therefore, if you only rely on grades as your assessment tool to gauge how you did as the course instructor, you won't capture the actual level of students' mastery (or your instructional skill). Use multiple assessment tools, and balance student grades against other forms of measurement.

Reflecting

One of the most important tasks you can do as an instructor is to spend time thinking about your class. You should be asking yourself questions such as, "Was that activity successful?" "How can I make that lesson stronger?" and "What is the best way to assess this learning?" These reflections should be ongoing as the semester and your course progress. Begin your reflections before the first class. If you have taught the class before, reflect on the activities and lessons that worked well and how your activities and lessons could be strengthened. If you have never taught before or have never taught the class, find out what other instructors are doing. Review course syllabi posted online. Talk to faculty who teach in your discipline and other disciplines as well.

It is critical to think about the flow of the class as the semester progresses. Have the lessons built upon each other? Is the information being presented in a way that encourages students to make important connections? It is better to make slight changes as you go along, than to wait until the end of the semester and realize that you did not achieve your goals and your students' outcomes were subpar.

We use course assessment file folders kept accessible all semester. As we teach, we add ideas, thoughts and keep a list of changes that need to be made to each course. Obviously, the file folder can exist digitally; your "notes" and observations may be kept conveniently in electronic format.

Before beginning to plan subsequent courses, that folder of ideas and reflections makes a reappearance as a resource. Reflecting on what did and didn't work as courses end, and having a quick source of new ideas, is a great way to constantly improve the course, student retention and success, as well as improve your own engagement.

While reflection should begin even before you teach the class, it should also be ongoing throughout the semester. Reflect after each class session, as well. Ask yourself questions such as: "Were my students engaged?" "Was I engaged?" and most importantly, "How can we make this class better?"

Those who have been teaching for a while know that each class has its own "personality." Because of the differences in class personalities, teaching is never a one size fits all affair. This is why having multiple ways to approach course content is important. For example, we have had classes populated with students who loved to work in groups and classes filled with students who preferred to work alone. Reflection and curation of ideas is an important step toward meeting the needs of your students and learning to leverage the "personalities" of your classes.

Student Surveys

"Having the opportunity to be a student in a very impressive flipped classroom semester-long group project, I will take the flexibility and humbleness that I've acquired with me into future internships and jobs. I got the chance to have a relationship with the students and teachers on a level above just coming to class and listening to a lecture. I will take these lessons learned and continue to grow in the future. For any students contemplating whether to take a flipped class or not, I would definitely say go for it. You have the opportunity to interact with your teachers and class members in such a fun way" (Perry, H., 2015).

An important part of this reflective process is to listen to your students. Sometimes you may conclude you are not reaching your students and have to focus on how to better engage them. Instead of groping around in the dark, trying to figure out how to find the right mix of activities for your classroom, distribute an anonymous survey to your students. Most LMS systems have this feature available, but if not hand out paper surveys in class and leave the room. Assign a student to collect them (to maintain anonymity of participants) and return them to you.

Remember that you are gathering information, not apologizing or laying blame for problems. Use this type of survey at the semester midpoint, even if the course is progressing well:

- It is a quick way to get feedback from the students;

- It can help you to avoid potential problems;

- It can help the students gain a feeling of control over their own education;

- It can bring to light new ideas or ways to approach course content.

One Minute Notes

These can be anonymous or you can require students to put their names on them. Ask a simple question the last five minutes of class and have the students write their answers to the prompt. You may ask students to identify three concepts or facts they learned, or to identify a course concept they are confused about. This gives you ongoing feedback about your class.

Student Evaluations

As you reflect on how well you achieved your goals, look at notes you made about the class as it was delivered. Look at student grades and think about the overall level of student engagement in class. In addition, look carefully at your student evaluations.

Most colleges offer end-of-class student evaluations for students to complete. Student evaluations incorporate closed-ended questions and some open-ended questions. The results are tabulated and emailed to the instructor, the department chair and the dean at the beginning of the following semester. We feel that student evaluations can be helpful in course planning in many ways.

Once the evaluations are deployed and available to our students, we spend class time explaining the importance of these evaluations. We emphasize the fact that they are anonymous and that we do not get the results until after final grades have been submitted. To further encourage participation, we make this an assignment, assigning a very small number of points to the activity. Because it is anonymous, we ask students to show us the screen that says that the evaluation has been submitted for the class. We also request that students tell us which activities they felt were helpful and which ones they felt were not on the surveys. We emphasize that changes are made to our classes based on their feedback.

One important point to remember is to not overuse survey instruments. If you overdo the surveys, students will stop taking them seriously. One survey in the middle of the semester and one at the end are usually about right. Use of the one minute notes can be done more often, even weekly. The important thing to remember is that you are asking your students to give you their time and effort. Be judicious of your requirements on their time. It is more important to engage with the subject matter than to answer repeated surveys. Finally, it is important to share the results of the survey with the students if you can. Explain the changes that will be made due to their input. Ask for clarification on anything you do not understand. Whatever you do, include the students in all steps of this process as much as you can.

Engagement (Yours and Theirs)

Reflecting on your engagement will reinvigorate your teaching. Lectures grow stale and memorized lectures rarely come from a place of passion. The weight of pulling students through a semester of coursework will wear down even the most enthusiastic faculty member. By blending our classes, we share the responsibility for learning with our students. Each class we teach offers the opportunity for innovation and critical thinking. Each class challenges us. This is exciting and allows us to share our love of our disciplines with our students on a whole new level.

Our increased engagement motivates us. This motivation helps us create classes that filled up quickly. Many of our students return to take other classes with us and they tell their friends to take classes with us. Blending allows us to maintain our passion for our work, and the students show their appreciation by signing up and completing our classes.

Student engagement is another aspect of your classroom performance that needs to be reflected upon. There are many ways that students show they are engaged. They come to class prepared to work. They ask questions and volunteer information in class. Of course not all students want to speak up in class. Make sure that you allow these students to engage in other ways. This could be through writing, audio recordings, videos or having an email or instant messaging conversation with the student about the course content.

After reflecting, analyze the data you have about your class. This includes final grades. If you taught this class before, do you see any changes in your final grades? In your blended course, expect an overall increase in final grades. Motivated students do better academically. How many students completed your class with average or below average grades? Identify the issues that may have contributed to poor student outcomes.

Examine your retention rates. How many students completed your class? Was there a point in the class when you lost multiple students? If so, what were you teaching at that point? Is there something you can do to make those parts of the class more user-friendly? Has your retention rate improved? How does your retention compare to department standards?

It is important to remember that teaching a blended acourse will require regular tweaking. You will regularly identify course materials, strategies, lesson plans and learning outcome goals that can be made stronger. New technology and world events will give you a constant stream of ideas that can be incorporated in your class. Just when you think you have your class in a really good place, your department will adopt a new textbook, and you will have to make necessary changes. There will always be new challenges. This is the nature of active learning and dynamic teaching.

While you are assessing your success, talk to others. Have a conversation with your chair or dean to verify that your courses and student outcomes are meeting the needs, goals and objectives of the department. Talk with others who teach. If you have a lesson that works really well, offer to share it. This type of sharing can open doors to a wide support network that can help you to be even more successful as you blend and flip your courses.

Visit your college's teaching and learning center. Particularly as an adjunct, it helps to seek out this resource. You may be surprised at what types of professional development are available to you. If you come from a small school, with limited resources, you may need to be a little more creative in your quest for support. Look at your professional organization to see if it offers any training that can help you. The more you learn about teaching and teaching methodology, the stronger you will be at your craft.

 Keep in mind that teaching, no matter how skilled the instructor, is not always an amazing, perfect experience. There will be days when things go wrong. When this happens, take a bit of a break and try not to beat yourself up. Understand that everyone has a bad moment or a bad class. Treat such situations as opportunities to learn from your mistakes and mix-ups.

Part IV
Blending Courses At
Any Level

CHAPTER 13
BLENDING LOWER-LEVEL, MID-LEVEL AND
UPPER-LEVEL SCIENCE COURSES

Democratizing Science Through Blending

For most students, introductory courses must be completed prior to advanced coursework because the courses are prerequisites. Because of the introductory nature of a course such as General Chemistry I, the course is often referred to as a "gateway course." The term "gateway" can imply a welcoming attitude; the majestic grandeur of the Gateway Arch in St. Louis might be envisioned—students pass in awe as they enter a new frontier of knowledge. As a teacher of introductory courses, envision yourself as a park ranger offering insights about the land beyond the gateway.

"Gate keeper" is often used to describe science courses as if the goal were to ward off any prospective students without the necessary cognitive skills to handle the demands of scientific content. What you want to try to avoid is the vision of a gated community, where students wait at the gate trying desperately to figure out the access code. You're not a sentry, imposing and imperial, conveying to your student that entry to the community is closely-guarded. Don't make your introductory course more cognitively difficult than necessary; this is pedagogically regressive.

In a study that examined which aspects of college helped students succeed (Chambliss and Takacs, 2014), the researchers interviewed 100 students and evaluated their educational trajectories at an unnamed institution. Undergraduates were more likely to major in a field if an introductory course were taught by an inspiring and caring faculty member. Students were also equally likely to write off an entire academic field if they had a *single negative experience* with a professor. The evidence is clear: caring, inspiring faculty make an enormous difference in the academic choices of college students.

Introductory courses impact the largest number of students. This is why large-enrollment, introductory courses may be the single most important types of courses to consider for a blended design.

The goal of this chapter is to provide a hands-on guide to generate more learning. The subtext is that if we educate a greater number of science students, then we democratize science education: we will provide millions of undergraduate students with opportunities to effectively learn in difficult courses so that the greatest possible number of students are provided a gateway into those science disciplines.

Introductory Courses

A staple of an undergraduate major is the large-enrollment introductory course sequence. In most instances the first course in a sequence is labeled as Chemistry I, Physics I, and Biology I. Often these courses are offered in two part although there are exceptions (calculus-based physics is usually offered as a three-semester sequence and biology can be offered in several formats) most courses include a laboratory component.

Use Pre-Assessments

The first week of your course sets the tone. A positive attitude about the course on your part can be infectious for your students. A well-organized blended course that promises to support learning through a variety of online resources can instill confidence in your students.

Remember the Dunning-Kruger effect from the last chapter? Your students may not be aware of their academic limitations. They may think that because they have already taken chemistry in high school, that an introductory chemistry course will be easy. This is why you need to know where your students stand with respect to basic scientific knowledge and basic math and science skills. Plan an online assessment given before the first class (or required by the start of the second class). It will generate useful data to help you shape your learning goals and fine tune your lesson plans.

Always remember that introductory students will arrive in your class with a variety of academic, social and socioeconomic backgrounds. Pre-assessments will improve student success and instructor satisfaction.

Give students skills pre-quizzes. Based on the results, dive deeper into each skill. For instance, mathematical skills are necessary for success in introductory chemistry and physics courses. So when teaching a blended introductory science course, plan a pre-course assessment that includes mathematics problems requiring skills that are needed for that particular course: fractions, logarithms, trigonometric functions and basic algebra.

Another crucial skill that can stymie many an introductory science student is exponential notation. The difficulty that students sometimes have in using their calculators will surprise you. Ask your students to enter the numbers for a calculation such as "4 x 6.02E23 = ?" Such explicit instruction in a pre-assessment exercise will often correct mistakes before students make them in an assignment or exercise.

Here are some other ideas for assessing and reviewing basic skills in your introductory science courses:

- Create mini-movies to review basic scientific and mathematical skills.

- Post the files for each skill on the LMS with instructions for students to review each presentation.

- Create skill-based screencasts (These may be reused for mid-level and upper level courses, as well).

Lesson planning and course goals based on pre-assessments, give students the metacognitive tools to master the course materials more effectively.

Technology for Introductory Courses

Integrating technology into your introductory course creates excitement and encourages students to log onto the course web site to complete assignments. In introductory courses that are blended, there are many opportunities to use technology to support student review of difficult concepts. Let's start with screencasting. It has been mentioned repeatedly this book because of its utility to provide students with succinct explanations of challenging content virtually on demand. Similarly, you can use a whiteboard in class to help students capture the explanation of a difficult scientific concept. When the white board images and the audio are captured, students have a resource to review out-of-class (see Chapter 10).

Another exciting technological tool for use in introductory blended science courses is the creation of interactive exercises. In General Chemistry, for example, course modules address challenging concepts such as balancing chemical equations, stoichiometry, limiting reagent calculations, and precipitation reactions. Students see such exercises more like games than assignments. The more time students spend on learning concepts, the more likely content information will move into long-term memory. Here's a list of interactive exercises available online for general chemistry courses:

• Mahjong Chem (http://www2.stetson.edu/mahjongchem/): Clear away the tiles while testing your knowledge of polyatomic ions, oxidation numbers, element symbols, and more.

• Periodic Table Battleship (http://teachbesideme.com/periodic-table-battleship/?hootPostID=898af3f453652a1381d0188f56 267bfa): You sank my... elements? Familiarize yourself with the periodic table when you turn it into the game board for this classic game.

• Adventures in Chemistry Games (https://www.acs.org/ content/acs/en/education/whatischemistry/adventures-in-chemistry/games.html): Join the molecule chase as you navigate the maze to escape Space Station Seven and save the world!

• Balancing Chemical Equations Game (http://phet.colorado. edu/sims/html/balancing-chemical-equations/latest/balancing-chemical-equations_en.html): Take the PhET challenge. Can you complete all three levels?

- Element Hangman (http://education.jlab.org/elementhang-man/prob665.html): Guess the name of the element before your atom man completely decays.

- Chemistry Games (http://www.mansfieldct.org/schools/mms/staff/hand/chemgames.htm): Who wants to be a matter million-aire? Can you reach the top level without using up your hints?

- Periodic Table Bingo (https://www.michigan.gov/documents/explorelabscience/Periodic_Table_Bingo_403152_7.pdf): BINGO! BINGO! Sorry, got carried away. You will too, as you learn about elements using this classic game with a periodic table twist.

 Encouraging time on task is pedagogically useful, but don't create assignment after assignment to fill students' time. Balance is required. Ask students about the interactive assignments to gauge the effectiveness of exercises.

Blended General Chemistry

General Chemistry, like Physics and Mathematics, involves a lot of problem solving that can be improved through practice. In a blended course, before class students review course material using a class guide or pre-class videos. During class, learners engage in problem-solving using clickers. After class—at the end of each week of material—learners engage with material via weekly online quizzes. The table on the following page outlines a typical week for a student in General Chemistry I on a Monday/Wednesday schedule with no class on Friday.

Day of the Week	Activity
Weekend	Read through the class guide consisting of PowerPoint slides or videos about the topic with learning goals for next week's class. Before class complete a pre-class assignment consisting of questions about the PowerPoint information and submit the assignment via a dropbox.
Monday	During class work in stable base groups to answer a series of clicker questions. Very little lecture occurs. Students are aided by the instructor and chemistry peer mentors who circulate throughout the room to assist with the problems.
Tuesday	If Wednesday's assignment was not completed over the weekend then turn it in by midnight.
Wednesday	Repeat Monday

Figure 13.1: Lesson Schedule

While Learning Objectives are necessary for every course, they are especially important for an introductory blended course. Students should start their pre-class preparation by understanding the LOs.

Class Time Management

As we have shown, managing class time is critically important in a blended course. One way to make the most of class time is to assign students to groups of four at the beginning of the semester. We often get asked about group composition in workshops. Group assignment may be done randomly, but grouping students by their majors works nicely. Try to ensure that no group contains a lone female. The literature on group composition in the classroom makes clear that a lone female often feels intimidated by the males in her group and is therefore less likely to participate.

Scaffolding

Two other important tools related to efficient management of class time in introductory courses are scaffolding and peer mentors.

Here's an example of how scaffolding works: Scaffolding encourages learning by motivation and by building upon previously-learning information and newly-acquired concepts.

1. Start the day's lesson with the least cognitively-challenging questions. As with teaching any complex concept or skill, break up the learning into segments.

2. Use clickers. As the class period unfolds, clicker questions address basic questions at first then slowly incorporate more conceptually challenging information.

3. By the end of class period, students will be solving the most cognitively-demanding problems and questions.

Complicated topics such as limiting reagent problems are scaffolded over several days with review slides to help remind students what they learned previously about balancing reactions, stoichiometry, and excess reagents.

Make sure your clicker question bank contains more questions than necessary for some topics. Skip questions if the class understands the concept as judged by a high percentage (usually 85 percent or more) of students answering the questions correctly. Re-poll if the number of incorrect answers is low, say less than 60 percent. You might decide to offer a mini-lecture on a topic or perhaps engage the class in a discussion about what issues arise during a given question. Clickers even allow a dissection of the question.

For example, for a limiting reactant problem, you can ask your class some of the following yes/no questions:

- Did you calculate the molar mass correctly for each of the necessary compounds? If many students say yes, ask which compound they calculated incorrectly. A question might be: Did you forget the "2" in H2?

- Did you know how to set up the problem?

- Did you use the correct stoichiometry between the two reagents (you could identify the two reagents)?

- Did you remember to subtract the amount used from the starting material when you determined the excess reagent?

Peer Mentors

Mentors are students who meet two criteria: they have successfully completed the course and they have strong interpersonal skills. Mentors do not need to have earned an "A" in the course, nor do they have to be naturally extroverted. The ratio of mentors to students should be 1:15 so that a typical course of 60 students would utilize four mentors. Make sure your mentors are well-trained: review course content with them and make sure they know how to ask open-ended questions. The goal of mentor training should be to ensure that the mentors learn how to facilitate learning.

Your mentors will circulate throughout the classroom during the entire class period. Mentoring improves student learning in the course, but a nice corollary effect is that mentors benefit from the experience (Amaral and Vala, 2009) as well.

Homework & Quizzes

Homework is the standard assignment for practice work to be completed after a traditional lecture. In your blended introductory course, homework still serves a useful purpose. Students rehearse material from class, reinforce concepts and are presented with multiple examples of the way problems may be worded.

Time on task should be your major consideration when designing homework assignments. The caveat with time on task relates to the amount of concentration that students expend on the task. Less is often more where homework is concerned. In General Chemistry I, for example, students should be given problems that have answers in the back of the textbook. You can grade the homework or just use it for practice so that your students do well on the next quiz.

Quizzes

Creating a quiz bank for a general chemistry course can be a time-consuming task. Be that as it may, academic integrity is a serious concern, so quizzes should be designed in such a way so that no student ever gets the same quiz. The creation of randomly-generated quizzes using banks of questions is possible through an LMS.

For the quizzes in General Chemistry I, you might create a quiz such as the one outlined below. The quiz focuses on information about nomenclature, the periodic table and formula weights. A representative question is included for each question. For question #2, as an example, there are 12 possible questions, each one a different element. When each student takes the quiz, only one of those 12 possible questions will be included. The same random generation occurs for every one of the questions on the quiz. Questions 15-17 are worth two points each on this quiz.

Figure 13.2: Quiz Questions

Question	Category	Representative Question
1	Periodicity of Elements	Which pair of elements below are the most similar in chemical properties?
2	Charges on Elements	Sodium forms an ion with a charge of ___.
3	Empirical formulae	Which compounds below do not have the same empirical formula?
4	Element determination	The formula of a salt is $XCl2$. The X-ion in this salt has 28 electrons. Metal X is _____.
5	Formula construction	Predict the empirical formula of the ionic compound that forms from sodium and fluorine.

6	Ionic formulae (mon-ovalent)	The correct formula for copper (II) chloride is _____ .
7	Ionic formula (multivalent)	The correct formula for mercury (II) phosphate is ____.
8	Acid formulae	The formula for phosphoric acid is _____ .
9	Covalent formulae	The correct name for SrO is _____ .
10	Ionic formulae I –write the name	The name of the ionic compound (NH4)3PO4 is _____ .
11	Ionic formulae II – write the name	The correct name for Al2(SO4)3 is _____ .
12	Ionic formulae III— transition metals	Nickel and chlorine form a compound with the formula NiCl2. The correct name for this compound is _____ .
13	Covalent formulae names	The correct name for CCl4 is _____.
14	Acid names	The correct name for HC2H3O2 is _____.
15	Balancing reactions I (four compounds)	When he following equation is balanced the coefficient of H2S is _____. (unbalanced reaction is given)
16	Balancing reactions II (four compounds)	When he equation is balanced the coefficient of H2O is _____. (unbalanced reaction is given)
17	Balancing reactions III (>four compounds)	When the equation is balanced the coefficient of CaCO3 is _____. (unbalanced reaction is given)

Permit students to use open books, open notes and open internet. This policy signals to students that they do not have to agonize over a quiz, and quizzes may be used as study tools. In a blended design, you should always be thinking of the pedagogical use of any assessment before you create the assessment.

Success in General Chemistry I is usually defined as a student earning a C or better in the course since a D does not count for most majors. At many institutions, the usual marker for success is to examine the DFW (D, F, or withdrawal) rate. The DFW rate for General Chemistry at Penn State Berks hovered around 50 percent. After launching a redesigned blended introductory general chemistry course, five years of student grades were analyzed. The DFW rate for the course dropped to under 30 percent. Not only did students experience more success in General Chemistry I, those who completed the course were more likely to succeed in General Chemistry II.

Physics

The more examples teachers have of blended courses, the more choices they will have when they opt to implement a blended course. Blending a physics course is done in much the same way you blended a chemistry course, because both disciplines are suffuse with problems created to help students master the material. In contemplating the physics classroom, the work of Eric Mazur merits careful attention. Mazur's work focuses on the use of clickers at Harvard: "In hindsight, the reason for my students' poor performance is simple. The traditional approach to teaching reduces education to a transfer of information (Mazur, 1997)."

Mazur's course offers enough contrast to the General Chemistry I course discussed earlier in this chapter to warrant analysis. Mazur opted to actively engage his students because of his own frustrations related to their poor performance, but then realized that the pedagogical literature included numerous reasons to make the changes he made. A remarkable study of 6,000 physics students (Hake, 1998), showed that instructors who employed some form of active learning in the course had significantly higher gains, as judged by the Force Concept Inventory (Hestenes et al., 1992). The inclusion of clickers during class time produced dramatic gains in student learning.

The importance of pre-class work is overlooked in the active learning literature. Yes, active learning produces dramatic gains and yes transmission of information is a poor pedagogical model, but carefully constructed pre-class work can help prepare students for the type of clicker questions that Mazur promotes.

ConcepTests

If Mazur's model incorporated more pre-class work, his model would be more closely allied with a blended design. Mazur estimated that he could cover roughly four major concepts in one 60-minute class period. He allots about two-thirds of the time for lecture and one-third for clicker questions (what he, and others, refer to as ConcepTests). A blended design would focus virtually the entire class period on ConcepTests and the lecture would be moved to the web for students to watch before the class period. Sample ConcepTests are listed below. The exciting part of the ConcepTests is that students do not need equations to solve them.

Think fast! You've just driven around a curve in a narrow, one-way street at 25 mph when you notice a car identical to yours coming straight toward you at 25 mph. You have only two options: hitting the other car head-on or swerving into a massive concrete wall, also head on. In the split second before the impact, you decide to:

1. Hit the other car
2. Hit the wall
3. Hit either one—it makes no difference
4. Consult your lecture notes

A compact car and a large truck collide head on and stick together. Which vehicle undergoes the larger acceleration during the collision?

1. Car
2. Truck
3. Both experience the same acceleration
4. Can't tell without knowing he velocity of the combined mass

By shaking one end of a stretched string, a single pulse is generated. The travelling pulse carries:

1. Energy

2. Momentum

3. Energy and momentum

4. Neither of the two

Figure 13.3: Sample ConcepTest

The curiosity aroused by questions such as these tap into the basic human desire to understand the world. If a physics instructor simply tells students that a single pulse contains both energy and momentum, the impact on cognition is not nearly as strong. The ConcepTests questions activate parts of the brain that are not activated by a statement. The simple act of asking a question, then, is one of the most powerful reasons to incorporate clickers into your blended courses.

Mazur relies heavily on the textbook, and the use of a textbook is still important in a science course. However, the time may soon come when textbooks are replaced by web-based lectures and notes. Certainly, most textbooks are now available in electronic format.

Biology

Introductory Biology differs from chemistry and physics because of its narrative nature: biology courses rely on stories rather than problems. The online quiz included in the General Chemistry section would be much more challenging to write for a section of biology. There are only so many organelles in a cell, for example, and creating a quiz bank of many different questions based on similar cognitive skills is challenging. In physics, one need only change the numbers in a problem to create a unique question. In biology, the number of quantitative problems is much smaller.

A more narrative discipline like Biology affords opportunities in a blended design to utilize class time engaged in activities that build conceptual understanding. We have always sympathized with our biology colleagues, because this discipline requires the most creativity of the three main introductory sciences. As explained above, physics and chemistry are older sciences with a well-established quantitative base. While we do not want to claim that teaching physics or chemistry is easy, the semester-long format in these two disciplines follows a fairly predictable formula: introduce a topic, expose students to the mathematical equations used to understand that topic, then spend class time going through carefully scaffolded problem sets to build understanding. Writing test questions in physics and chemistry requires less creativity than in biology: when you can change a chemical, a slope, a speed, a charge, a field, or any other parameter in a problem multiple problems are easier to construct.

What type of activities can students complete in class? Labeling the parts of a cell and then thinking of creative metaphors for each of the organelles; thinking of creative ecosystems that would facilitate a certain a type of life; genetics worksheets using Punnet squares; dissecting family trees; translation worksheet to determine the amino acid sequence of a given piece of DNA or RNA. Creating activities can be enjoyable and students often have an extra jolt of motivation if the activity has never been tried before.

The time spent on classroom activities can be generated by carefully constructing the pre-class learning. A blended design enables increased creativity. Learners could spend time prior to class watching short, introductory screen capture videos combined with learning tools such as definition sheets, summary pages of classification schemas, and labeled images. Students might be directed to print a particular sheet and bring it to class. A given classification scheme could be used as a model for in-class activities where specific segments of the classification are explored in more depth.

After-class activities may be extensions of in-class activities that can lead into the next class session. The blending of pre- and post-class work is especially exciting because students merge their learning across all three learning opportunities (before, during and after class). As with physics and chemistry online quizzes can motivate time on task. The quizzes could be daily, weekly, or by topic. The decisions about quizzes should align with what the objectives for quizzing.

Mid-Level/Upper-Level Courses

The Focus on Cognitive Skills

Courses beyond the introductory level present unique challenges. The goals of mid-level coursework are to serve as a bridge between the introductory material and the upper-level coursework. Upper-level courses are often terminal, i.e., students do not need the information for subsequent courses. Students taking mid-level and upper-level courses are, by default, more mature learners and therefore may not need the same kind of support provided in introductory courses. You will have transfer students who took introductory courses elsewhere, and you will have students who placed out of the introductory courses, e.g., via AP exams.

The content of these courses focuses on cognitive skills on higher rungs of Bloom's Taxonomy. There will still be knowledge and comprehension, but now you will help students *apply their knowledge and analyze concepts.*

In upper-level courses, focus on critical thinking—at least some of the cognitive tasks should be at the level synthesis and evaluation. Projects and papers, as well as the collaborative projects discussed in Chapter 9 are ideal for junior/senior level courses. Formative assessment associated with blended courses will facilitate more meta-cognition: you want to help students think more deeply about how they learn and gauge if they are both "on the right track" and "up to snuff" with their contemporaries.

One way to get students centered on a big question, is to start with reasonable pre-knowledge. Grab students' attention with a current event or a controversial topic. By stimulating their thinking, your students start to access prior knowledge which facilitates deeper thinking about the topic.

A pertinent example is climate change. Whether it be understanding the effects of fossil fuels on atmosphere, or the degree of change that needs to happen now to reverse the potential damage already set in motion, understanding climate change will require the student to understand the complex set of scientific mechanisms that brought us to this point. Disregard their personal biases, and concentrate instead on the chemical, biological, or climatological aspects being discussed. By assigning environmental literature, you can prime your students' pre-knowledge pumps and promote lively, informed, face-to-face meetings that are not only fun but focus on your learning objectives and goals.

We have witnessed this approach implemented in a large systems biology class (>200 students). The instructor skillfully assigned a set of documents to the even numbered sections of the class and another set to the odd numbered sections. Like every good blender, he included a small clicker quiz to start the class in order to reinforce that students should come prepared. He used it throughout the face-to-face time to illustrate the pertinent aspects of the argument. Because the class had been assigned two different readings, the debate was rich and the comments genuine as their pre-knowledge came from different perspectives. The peer-to-peer learning was evident.

In the last five minutes of class, he wrapped up the debate, highlighted what was spoken about and related it to the learning objectives of the day and how those related to the course objectives.

Here's another example of how to reiterate early scientific principles while simultaneously moving mid- and upper-level students' thinking to higher levels of Bloom's Taxonomy through knowledge creation. It involves a play on "problem-based learning," which is transformed into "disease-based learning."

In a blended "medical sciences" course, the instructor chose a number of societal diseases and treatments to explore with the students. Through careful choices of topics and multiple group and individual pre-knowledge exercises, she helped her class demonstrate that science is in a constant state of flux. Among her learning outcomes (LOs) was to help students hone their presentation skills. Surrounding each particular pathology in question, students identified and demonstrated how biological, physiological, and anatomical approaches continue to change with technologies.

This instructor's year long capstone class shows a great integration of basic science courses with modern disease states: the course changes from year-to-year to keep up with the development of new chemotherapy or diagnostic criteria.

Upper-Level Courses: Different But Similar

If you teach upper-level coursework, you'll experience more control over what to cover, because most upper-level courses are not prerequisites. You can expect more from students, but don't think of an upper-level course learning outcomes and instructional goals as fundamentally different from any other level course.

In an upper-level blended science course, you'll assign more projects, but you'll also spend time helping students scaffold prior information and connect it to the new information. Let's look at three considerations related to teaching upper-level blended courses in a bit more detail.

First, an upper-level course is not fundamentally different than any other course. This means that the same general ideas apply concerning the blending cycle. You still design work prior to class, use active learning in class, and create activities for students to complete after class.

 Upper-level course class size is usually smaller, so assign more student presentations. Don't forget written assignments such as a research paper that encourages students to synthesize information while also evaluating it.

In an upper-level class, the after class work will be more extensive. Assign projects such as the creation of a wiki page or the production of a short (<5 minutes) instructional video. Have students create public service announcements using technology. Second, instead of spending weeks reviewing information from previous courses in biology, chemistry, and physics, create activities so that students can self-assess their retention of such knowledge.

Help students learn to transfer information from previous courses and apply that information to the new material. Create out-of-class review work for students to work on more transfer skills.

For example, students might see enzyme kinetics in biochemistry, but not recall all the time they spend on kinetics in general chemistry. Create worksheets for students to help them access prior knowledge and you'll increase learning.

Lastly, upper-level coursework often allows you freedom. You can focus on designing pre-class, in-class and after-class lessons and assessments that target critical thinking. You'll also be able to vary the content from year to year as you find different topics to help students understand the nature of scientific thought.

CHAPTER 14
COURSES FOR NON-SCIENCE MAJORS

Helping a non-science major better understand the specialized knowledge associated with a particular field of study can be intensely gratifying. Blending a non-major course is especially important, because you will encounter a wider range of student ability than in a course for majors. Non-majors courses rarely have pre-requisites, so anyone can enroll. Blending will meet the unique challenges associated with helping non-majors to learn science.

In a general education course, you might be hoping to change minds as well as imparting content knowledge. If you're teaching a non-majors course, *Engaging Ideas* (Bean, 2011) is the book to read. "Part Three" is especially valuable. Think about your science course for non-majors more like a liberal arts course. You want students to be able to write about scientific ideas and read difficult texts.

Teach Non-Majors Differently

Try to avoid textbooks in the usual sense and encourage students to read more broadly, e.g., newspapers (Mysliwiec et al., 2003) and science popularizations (Shibley et al., 2008). Give students plenty of opportunity to look at the big picture and to connect the scientific knowledge that they already have to new knowledge.

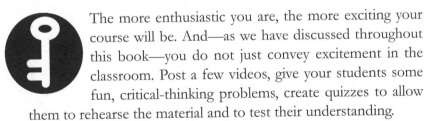 The more enthusiastic you are, the more exciting your course will be. And—as we have discussed throughout this book—you do not just convey excitement in the classroom. Post a few videos, give your students some fun, critical-thinking problems, create quizzes to allow them to rehearse the material and to test their understanding.

Since you are not bound by specific concepts beyond what the course catalog prescribes, you can creatively tie in concepts to topics the students choose. If you really want to try something exciting allow students to vote on the topics that you'll cover. More than any other course you'll teach, a non-majors course can be the most fun. Enjoy it...and your students will too.

Before, During and After

Before

When planning a non-majors course, use the same blended design format. You want to activate student interest in the subject matter before they come into the classroom. Design worksheets, surveys or quizzes to help introduce the subject so that class time may be spent interacting with the content and providing time for students to learn from each other. Remember to structure online work after class to help keep your students working between class sessions.

An important goal of a non-majors course is to motivate students to want to learn your subject. You need to conceive of interesting ways to help illuminate the subject. Students like stories so find stories about the subject matter you're teaching. Weave those stories through your in-class activities. Below, you'll find two examples of courses for non-majors.

During—Biochemistry: Understanding the Bases of Human Disease

Consider a course designed to provide a window into the field of biochemistry. Let's call it BIOCHEM 001. When choosing a textbook for a course like this, use a slimmed-down version of a text used for a majors course. Textbook representatives may encourage you to adopt an expensive mini-version of what you might call a "majors-in-miniature" course. You might instead use a scientific popularization text. In the case of a non-majors biochemistry course, you might choose *Full Catastrophe Living: Using the Wisdom of Your Body and Mind to Face, Stress, Pain, and Illness* (Kabat-Zinn and Hanh, 2009) or *How We Die* (Nuland, 1994). Integrating this type of text provides the student encouragement you want. Then, your job is to fill in the scientific details.

Whether using a science popularization or a condensed textbook, the goals remain the same:

- introduce information prior to class (perhaps by asking questions about the assigned reading)

- use class time for active-learning activities that engage your students

- give students post-class assignments to help them consolidate the content knowledge

- create writing assignments

After—Astronomy

An implicit conception of the design of general education science courses is that the course should excite the learner. A goal of the pedagogy should be that the learner leaves the course wanting to continue to explore the subject after the course ends. A question that is often asked on assessment instruments is whether the student would be more likely to read a newspaper article about the subject after completing the course. The biochemistry course described above tries to lure students into the subject by focusing on diseases. The description for the University of Pittsburgh course "Stonehenge to Hubble" contains much information that helps drive the pedagogy.

"This is a self-contained course for students not majoring in the physical sciences. Lectures focus on practical astronomy and provide a historical perspective of our place in the Universe. Phenomena that can be readily observed with the unaided eye or a small telescope are discussed. The historical perspective starts with the earliest views, and discusses scientific discovery as a process leading up to the modern idea of the expanding universe of galaxies. Part of this course includes the requirement of up to two evening "field trips" to the University of Pittsburgh's Allegheny Observatory. The purpose of these trips will be to tour the facility and, if possible, make observation with a telescope. On any one evening only a small fraction of the class will make a trip, so it should be possible to accommodate the students' evening schedules. Nominally, the trips will take place on a Tuesday or Wednesday evening. Bus transportation from the Oakland campus to the Observatory will be provided. A small percentage of the course grade will be based on participation in these field trips."

From the first-line of the description, the type of learner is delineated. A concern with such a description begins with the first word of the second sentence. Must the teacher lecture? Can lecture occur online or does the term "lecture" imply seat time in a classroom? Some encouraging goals include "scientific discovery as a process" and the requirement of field trips. The notion of active learning in the field trips could prove to be a memorable learning experience but the trips will have to be woven into the course design in pedagogically useful ways.

CHAPTER 15
BLENDED LABORATORY LEARNING

Science courses provide an opportunity to apply each discipline in a practical environment. As an educator, you inherently know the importance of these experiential exercises but you are often caught in ruts, redoing what others have done or repeating the same practices. If you teach a course that has a laboratory component this might be the best place to start blending. Laboratory design is not as entrenched as the perceptions of lecture course design. Let's consider how a blended design might work.

All too often we see students enter this environment completely unprepared for the experience. Sometimes their lab books are pristine and it is obvious that absolutely no pre-work was done. The lack of preparation is pedagogically disastrous: the student arrives without direction and floats in the lab. Despite your best intention with clear learning objectives and lab instructions, the student will learn little.

Yes, You Can Blend Labs

By nature, laboratories are social environments; students often work in groups. The collaborative environment provides a great opportunity to learn from others and not just in class. To maximize collaboration, all students should arrive equally prepared. One way to accomplish this is to hold students accountable through pre-class work. For example, require group members work together to submit a group pre-lab. This suggestion should sound familiar at this point. But in our workshops, laboratory work is usually the one place that teachers think that blending will not work.

A blended laboratory design helps ensure that the students arrive with reasonable levels of pre-knowledge surrounding both the laboratory practical implications. You want to introduced safety practices, equipment to use, lab procedures for the day as well as the learning objectives for that lab. Through creative pre-work work, you can propel students to greater understanding of the tasks at hand.

As with other type of courses, pre-class videos can help. By creating videos you accomplish two broad goals: first you illustrate how students can succeed in the lab and second, you get students thinking about the lab prior to walking into the physical space. The first goal demonstrates the culture and the meta-cognitive understanding of how "stuff" is to work. The second goal helps students focus on the tasks for the day and how to achieve them—you help them learn what we call skills. When lab culture and lab skills align with expectations, students are better able to achieve learning objectives.

Let's talk about culture for a moment and use Gross Anatomy Lab as an example. In any laboratory environment, there are a set of cultural practices that need to be adhered to for safety. Often we stress where the fume hood is, the fire extinguishers, the eye wash stations etc. and that is fine but getting to the cultural sides of why accidents or gaffs occur can often avoid the mishap in the first place. In gross anatomy, discretion and teamwork are big components of our learning exercises.

Gross Anatomy

Before students ever get to the first lab you should ensure that students have watched the pre-class videos that underlie these principles. Layer cultural principles into the student's first experience in the lab so that the shock of cadaveric dissection can be minimized. In the first lab you might have a memorial to honor those who've given us their bodies. The pre-class work should introduce appropriate behavior and then at the start of class you need to reiterate those behaviors. The pre-class work should help inculcate a level of respect. The pre-class work can also review skills necessary for success in the cadaver lab. Your students will then start building those skills before they ever lift their first scalpel

By creating space prior to class for students to interact with lab culture, lab skills, and lab protocols you set the stage before any "real" lab work begins. The cultural aspect of being a scientists, a member of a community, may be one of the most overlooked aspects of laboratory work and can make or break the learning experiences for students. We encourage you to consider the type of learning community you want so that you can better prepare students for success as a member of that community.

The skills necessary for laboratory success are often demonstrated in the physical space of the laboratory. You can save time in the laboratory by encouraging skill development prior to lab time. You want to help connect your students' growing disciplinary knowledge to the laboratory. By helping them reflect on skills, you help them bring more of that disciplinary knowledge to life. When a student doesn't understand why they are doing precipitation reactions in a general chemistry laboratory it's harder to get them to care.

It would be hard for a student to dissect the scapula if they were unsure where it was and how it was connected to the surrounding structures. It would be equally hard if they didn't know the scalpel doesn't arrive in hand with the blade, in fact one must manually put this together and if not done correctly, cuts will definitely happen. The same could be said for pipetting, it's not a natural thing in most students lives so why not give them a quick tour virtually on your LMS prior so that you don't have to stop somebody from mouth pipetting the HCl! These quick "How-to" vignettes can be housed in your course or laboratory LMS directory and students can go back to them as required or even on the fly should a rebuff be required. If it is an important skill and the laboratory has a graded component, one could easily reinforce and reward students for good behaviors by using some low-stake quizzes to internalize these skills.

Finally, the most critical skill sets grow when a student's disciplinary knowledge interacts with her/his practical laboratory experiences. Of course, you will discuss in detail the basic "pieces" of disciplinary knowledge in the face-to-face sections of the class. You can also provide a quick overview of the learning objectives of the laboratory. Highlights the anatomy, equipment, or point out pitfalls to avoid. Illustrate at a high level how all of the aspects of the lab fit together. A video easily complements the laboratory manual. If you have laboratory or teaching assistants, conduct a short pre-lab exercise to make sure that everyone communicates the same materials to students. Exposing assistants to this approach helps them understand the pedagogic process and helps shape their own teaching philosophies.

In many of our own past labs, we chose to administer one or two multiple choice exams that comprised a major part of the lab grade. In addition, we wrote up laboratory reports in the scientific method for our laboratory and/or teaching assistants. These are excellent cumulative exercises, and as you develop your skills at blending your laboratory environments you will also understand the power of teamwork and discussion. If laboratories enable problem-based approaches that may not have a clear yes, no, or $1/n-(x+2)$ answer, students engage in more complex thinking. They start to understand the greater nuances of the science at hand and develop meta-cognitive approaches that help them learn the materials. Students learn to tackle apparent ambiguity, but do so with less stress. Yes, these are lofty goals of the lowly lab, but they can be achieved with re-thinking lesson goals, approaches and by applying the principles of blended learning.

Of course, in some disciplines, the ability to leave the confines of the laboratory is not only expected, it's required. Personal biological field studies, geological field trips, or studying the effects of modern sprawl on local ecosystems will all be brought immediately to life outside the confines of walls. Blending a lab might mean leaving the confines of the lab behind. Here, with the power of mobile devices students can be lead to areas where you'd like them to use their observational prowess to study the particular phenomenon in question.

During a teaching conference, we witnessed one person who used Google Street View to orientate students to particular places in their town. The instructor uploaded turn of the 20th-century photographs at particular locations where students could easily examine the modern landscape and juxtapose this current view to what was once there. This is a nice form of augmented reality laboratory that combined historical records. As the world of big data comes closer to personal mobile computing, this type of laboratory can be done by accessing governmental databases for city planning, maps, soil sampling topographic maps, etc. The list is only as limited as your imagination, so don't confine the experience only to the classroom. You will enjoy the process and your students will benefit enormously.

The laboratory is a place to experience the science. Science faculty often repeat the exact processes and exercises that we completed as undergraduate and graduate students, but by leveraging the strategies of blending, it should become obvious that the sky is the limit. When you give your students the opportunity to leverage the power of pre-knowledge to gain both lab culture and lab skills prior to setting foot in the lab, this increases the learning potential of the lab experience.

As science teachers, one of our goals is for science students to concentrate on the principles *of* the science rather than struggling with how to *do* the science. Blended labs will help you accomplish this goal.. By incorporating pre-knowledge with communication in the lab, your students will be learn to integrate their newly-found practical knowledge into face-to-face environments. The practical science knowledge you teach them, will become a permanent part of your students' cycle of learning.

CHAPTER 16
PROFESSIONAL DEVELOPMENT: GROWING AS A TEACHER

You've covered a lot of territory in this book. You've read a summary of the neurobiology of learning, an outline of the five descriptors for blending (Balanced, Learner-Centered, Engagement Driven, Novel and Dynamic) and explored the blended cycle (before, during, and after). You've read about various technologies that support blended learning and seen those blended learning strategies in action in a variety of science courses. As we near the end of our exploration of blending learning in collegiate science classrooms, you may be wondering "What's next?"

You're next. You're reading this book, because you're interested in blending a science course. This book provides a launch pad and it lays the foundation for your development as an instructor interested in blended learning, but your learning has just begun.

The book *Outliers* introduces the concept of 10,000 hours (Gladwell, 2008). After researching people who had become experts in a variety of fields, the author calculated that it would take 10,000 hours of focused practice to develop expertise in an area. While this work focused on the work of hockey players and musicians, the concept applies to blended instruction as well. It's going to take practice and reflection to become a blending expert. Thankfully, you don't have to do it alone. There are lots of professional development opportunities that can help you grow as a blended instructor. Let's discuss a few.

Professional Organizations and Conferences

As you start your journey to become an expert blended instructor, you may want to join a professional organization that focuses on blended learning in collegiate environments or attend conferences. The International Association for Blended Learning (iabl.org) works to "promote excellence in teaching, training, and research in blended learning through the engagement of international scholars and practitioners to meet the needs of today's global learners." In addition to providing resources for blended instructors, the IABL organizes its annual Worldwide Conference on Blended Learning. The conference sessions span a variety of content areas, technologies and techniques.

Broadening the scope a bit, the Online Learning Consortium (OLC) bills itself as "the leading professional organization devoted to advancing quality online learning by providing professional development, instruction, best practice publications and guidance to educators, online learning professionals and organizations around the world." While the OLC encompasses the broader landscape of "online learning" and not just blended learning, blended instructors can find some valuable resources by joining the organization. The OLC also offers an annual OLC Innovate conference to support the development of innovative uses of technology in online, blended and hybrid environments.

Another professional organization that you may wish to explore is EDUCAUSE, a nonprofit association whose mission "is to advance higher education through the use of information technology." EDUCAUSE has several focus areas and initiatives that support the use of blended learning in collegiate settings. For instance, their EDUCAUSE Learning Initiative (ELI) is dedicated to promote innovations in learning through the integration of technology. The ELI partners each year with the New Media Consortium to publish its NMC Horizon Report which identifies emerging technologies and instructional strategies that are likely to have an impact in higher education settings. The ELI also holds a variety of events (webinars, online courses and conferences) to support the use of blended learning.

Outside of the conferences offered by these professional organizations, all of the major learning management systems (Blackboard, Brightspace, etc.) hold annual conferences that examine how the tools can be incorporated in face-to-face, blended and online learning environments. Attending these conferences can help you network with science instructors at other institutions who are using the same LMS to support their blended efforts. In addition to theses conferences, Magna Publications holds an annual Teaching with Technology conference that examines a wide-range of ways to integrate technology into face-to-face and online classes. (In full disclosure, all three authors have served on the Advisory Board for the Teaching with Technology conference which helps to select presenters, keynote speakers and conference strands.)

You can also find a lot of support for blended learning success by attending one of the broader teaching and learning conferences dedicated to institutions of higher education. For instance, while the *Teaching Professor* and POD Network conferences do not focus specifically on technology or blended instruction, recent programs from both conferences included sessions dedicated to blended course design.

Journals

When considering journals that can contribute to your growth as a blended science instructor, we recommend examining a disciplinary journal that highlights the scholarship of teaching and learning (SOTL) in your content area. For instance, the *Journal of Chemical Education* has regularly featured articles on hybrid and blended techniques for a variety of chemistry classroom environments. Similar results can be found in *The Physics Teacher*, *Anatomical Sciences Education* and the *Journal of Microbiology* and *Biology Education*. One of our favorites is *CBE* (*Cell Biology Education*). The journal features articles that have helped shape our own teaching. Disciplinary journals allow you to hear from colleagues who have blended their courses, or undertaken research concerning blended learning at other universities.

In addition to disciplinary journals, you should consider subscribing to professional newsletters. Magna Publications offers two monthly newsletter that directly applies to your work as a collegiate faculty member and developing blended instructor. *The Teaching Professor* focuses mainly on evidence-based practices in face-to-face settings but many of the strategies can inform your blended instruction. The company also publishes *Online Classroom* which examines emerging trends, challenges and strategies for effective online instruction. While the online component is only one part of the blended learning cycle; the newsletter can help you develop strategies to effectively balance the online and face-to-face portions of your blended classroom and identify novel ways to engage your students.

Teaching and Learning Centers

Your institution may offer additional professional development avenues for your growth as a blended instructor. Many colleges and universities have a Teaching and Learning Center (TLC) that organizes events and programs to assist with faculty development. While these centers go by a variety of names (Center for Academic Excellence, Center for Instructional Innovation, etc), they are designed to support your growth as an instructor. These centers can be a valuable source for information as you begin your journey as a blended instructor. You may also want to see whether your institution offers assistance with instructional design or the integration of educational technology. Many institutions of higher education have dedicated staff and departments to provide support for faculty with their online, face-to-face and blended learning efforts. This could be another valuable source for professional development.

Supporting Others

We have outlined avenues to support your growth as a blended instructor and it's important to remember the words from Isaac Newton: "If I have seen further it is by standing on the shoulders of giants."

As you develop unique instructional strategies and techniques to support your students' learning, you can provide the metaphorical shoulders upon which your colleagues can stand. Be willing to share your efforts and successes. Provide support for colleagues who want to try blending their classrooms. Look for opportunities to collaborate with colleagues who teach similar content and students. "[B]eing part of a nurturing community" is one of the prime motivators for professors (Wergin, 2001). As you develop your expertise as a blended instructor, reach out to other faculty members and support their growth. While this book provides you with a foundation for blending your science classroom, your progress (and those of your colleagues) will depend on what you do with this information.

COPYRIGHT FAIR USE GUIDELINES FOR COLLEGE FACULTY

Courtesy of the Stanford Copyright and Fair Use Center, Stanford University Libraries, Stanford University, 2017 (http://fairuse.stanford.edu/).

What Types of Creative Work Does Copyright Protect?

Copyright protects works such as poetry, movies, CD-ROMs, video games, videos, plays, paintings, sheet music, recorded music performances, novels, software code, sculptures, photographs, choreography and architectural designs.

To qualify for copyright protection, a work must be "fixed in a tangible medium of expression." This means that the work must exist in some physical form for at least some period of time, no matter how brief. Virtually any form of expression will qualify as a tangible medium, including a computer's random access memory (RAM), the recording media that capture all radio and television broadcasts, and the scribbled notes on the back of an envelope that contain the basis for an impromptu speech.

In addition, the work must be original — that is, independently created by the author. It doesn't matter if an author's creation is similar to existing works, or even if it is arguably lacking in quality, ingenuity or aesthetic merit. So long as the author toils without copying from someone else, the results are protected by copyright.

Permission: What Is It and Why Do I Need It?

Obtaining copyright permission is the process of getting consent from a copyright owner to use the owner's creative material. Obtaining permission is often called "licensing"; when you have permission, you have a license to use the work. Permission is often (but not always) required because of intellectual property laws that protect creative works such as text, artwork, or music. (These laws are explained in more detail in the next section.) If you use a copyrighted work without the appropriate permission, you may be violating—or "infringing"—the owner's rights to that work. Infringing someone else's copyright may subject you to legal action. As if going to court weren't bad enough, you could be forced to stop using the work or pay money damages to the copyright owner.

As noted above, permission is not always required. In some situations, you can reproduce a photograph, a song, or text without a license. Generally, this will be true if the work has fallen into the public domain, or if your use qualifies as what's called a "fair use." Both of these legal concepts involve quite specific rules. In most cases, however, permission is required, so it is important to never assume that it is okay to use a work without permission.

Many people operate illegally, either intentionally or through ignorance. They use other people's work and never seek consent. This may work well for those who fly under the radar—that is, if copyright owners never learn of the use, or don't care enough to take action.

Obtaining Clearance for Coursepacks

It is the instructor's obligation to obtain clearance for materials used in class. Instructors typically delegate this task to one of the following:

- Clearance services. These services are the easiest method of clearance and assembly.

- University bookstores or copy shops. University policies may require that the instructor delegate the task to the campus bookstore, copy shop, or to a special division of the university that specializes in clearances.

Using a Clearance Service

It can be time-consuming to seek and obtain permission for the 20, 30, or more articles you want to use in a coursepack. Fortunately, private clearance services will, for a fee, acquire permission and assemble coursepacks on your behalf. After the coursepacks are created and sold, the clearance service collects royalties and distributes the payments to the rights holders. Educational institutions may require that the instructor use a specific clearance service.

The largest copyright clearing service is the Copyright Clearance Center (www.copyright.com), which clears millions of works from thousands of publishers and authors.

In 2001, XanEdu (www.xanedu.com), acquired the coursepack service formerly known as Campus Custom Publishing. In addition to providing traditional coursepack assembly, XanEdu offers an electronic online service that provides supplemental college course materials directly to the instructor's desktop via the internet.

Educational Uses of Non-Coursepack Materials

Unlike academic coursepacks, other copyrighted materials can be used without permission in certain educational circumstances under copyright law or as a fair use. "Fair use" is the right to use portions of copyrighted materials without permission for purposes of education, commentary or parody.

The Code of Best Practices in Fair Use for Media Literacy Education

In 2008, the Center for Media and Social Impact, in connection with American University, unveiled a guide of fair use practices for instructors in K–12 education, in higher education, in nonprofit organizations that offer programs for children and youth, and in adult education. The guide identifies five principles that represent acceptable practices for the fair use of copyrighted materials. You can learn more at the center's website, (www.cmsimpact.org).

Guidelines Establish a Minimum, Not a Maximum

In a case alleging 75 instances of infringement in an educational setting, 70 instances were not infringing because of fair use and for other reasons. The infringements were alleged because of the posting of copyrighted books within a university's e-reserve system. The court viewed the Copyright Office's 1976 Guidelines for Educational Fair Use as a minimum, not a maximum standard. The court then proposed its own fair use standard—10% of a book with less than ten chapters, or of a book that is not divided into chapters, or no more than one chapter or its equivalent in a book of more than ten chapters.—*Cambridge University Press v. Georgia State University*, Case 1:08-cv-01425-OD (N.D. Ga., May 11, 2012).

What is the Difference Between the Guidelines and Fair Use Principles?

The educational guidelines are similar to a treaty that has been adopted by copyright owners and academics. Under this arrangement, copyright owners will permit uses that are outlined in the guidelines. In other fair use situations, the only way to prove that a use is permitted is to submit the matter to court or arbitration. In other words, in order to avoid lawsuits, the various parties have agreed on what is permissible for educational uses, codified in these guidelines.

What is an "Educational Use?"

The educational fair use guidelines apply to material used in educational institutions and for educational purposes. Examples of "educational institutions" include K-12 schools, colleges, and universities. Libraries, museums, hospitals, and other nonprofit institutions also are considered educational institutions under most educational fair use guidelines when they engage in nonprofit instructional, research, or scholarly activities for educational purposes.

"Educational Purposes" are:

• non-commercial instruction or curriculum-based teaching by educators to students at nonprofit educational institutions

- planned noncommercial study or investigation directed toward making a contribution to a field of knowledge, or

- presentation of research findings at noncommercial peer conferences, workshops, or seminars.

Rules for Reproducing Text Materials for Use in Class

The guidelines permit a teacher to make one copy of any of the following: a chapter from a book; an article from a periodical or newspaper; a short story, short essay, or short poem; a chart, graph, diagram, drawing, cartoon, or picture from a book, periodical, or newspaper.

Teachers may not photocopy workbooks, texts, standardized tests, or other materials that were created for educational use. The guidelines were not intended to allow teachers to usurp the profits of educational publishers. In other words, educational publishers do not consider it a fair use if the copying provides replacements or substitutes for the purchase of books, reprints, periodicals, tests, workbooks, anthologies, compilations, or collective works.

Rules for Reproducing Music

An instructor can make copies of excerpts of sheet music or other printed works, provided that the excerpts do not constitute a "performable unit," such as a whole song, section, movement, or aria. In no case can more than 10% of the whole work be copied and the number of copies may not exceed one copy per pupil. Printed copies that have been purchased may be edited or simplified provided that the fundamental character of the work is not distorted or the lyrics altered.

A student may make a single recording of a performance of copyrighted music for evaluation or rehearsal purposes, and the educational institution or individual teacher may keep a copy. In addition, a single copy of a sound recording owned by an educational institution or an individual teacher (such as a tape, disc, or cassette) of copyrighted music may be made for the purpose of constructing aural exercises or examinations, and the educational institution or individual teacher can keep a copy.

Rules for Recording and Showing Television Programs

Nonprofit educational institutions can record television programs transmitted by network television and cable stations. The institution can keep the tape for 45 days, but can only use it for instructional purposes during the first ten of the 45 days. After the first ten days, the video recording can only be used for teacher evaluation purposes, to determine whether or not to include the broadcast program in the teaching curriculum. If the teacher wants to keep it within the curriculum, he or she must obtain permission from the copyright owner. The recording may be played once by each individual teacher in the course of related teaching activities in classrooms and similar places devoted to instruction (including formalized home instruction). The recorded program can be repeated once if necessary, although there are no standards for determining what is and is not necessary. After 45 days, the recording must be erased or destroyed.

A video recording of a broadcast can be made only at the request of and only used by individual teachers. A television show may not be regularly recorded in anticipation of requests—for example, a teacher cannot make a standing request to record each episode of a PBS series. Only enough copies may be reproduced from each recording to meet the needs of teachers, and the recordings may not be combined to create teaching compilations. All copies of a recording must include the copyright notice on the broadcast program as recorded and (as mentioned above) must be erased or destroyed after 45 days.

References

Adams, P., Gingras, H. (2017) Blended Learning and Flipped Classrooms: A Comprehensive Guide, Part-Time Press, Ann Arbor, MI.

Abraham, Joel. K. (2009) 'Addressing Undergraduate Student Misconceptions about Natural Selection with an Interactive Simulated Laboratory,' Evolution Education and Outreach, Vol. 2, No. 3, pp. 393-404.

Allen, D. & Tanner, K. (2006) 'Rubrics: Tools for Making Learning Goals and Evaluation Criteria Explicit for Both Teachers and Learners', CBE - Life Sciences Education, Vol. 5, No. 3, pp.197-203.

Allen, I. E., Seaman, J., Poulin, R. & Strautt, T. T. (2016) Online Report Card: Tracking Online Education in the United States. Babson Park, MA: Babson Survey Research Group and Quahog Research Group, LLC.

Amaral, K. E. & Shank, J. D. (2010) 'Enhancing Student Learning and Retention with Blended Learning Class Guides', Educause Quarterly, Vol. 33, No. 4, pp.0.

Amaral, K. E. & Vala, M. (2009) 'What Teaching Teaches: Mentoring and the Performance Gains of Mentors', Journal of Chemical Education, Vol. 86, No. 5, pp.630.

Ambrose, S. A., Bridges, M. W., Dipietro, M., Lovett, M. C. & Norman, M. K. (2010) How learning works: Seven research-based principles for smart teaching, ed., John Wiley & Sons.

American Test Anxiety Association, http://amtaa.org/.

Anderson, L. W. & Krathwohl, D. R. (2001) A Taxonomy for Learning, Teaching, and Assessing: A Revision of Bloom's Taxonomy of Educational Objectives, ed., Addison Wesley Longman, Inc., New York.

Angelo, T. A. & Cross, K. P. (1993) 'Classroom assessment techniques', Vol., No.

Barr, R. B. & Tagg, J. (1995a) 'From Teaching to Learning: A New Paradigm for Undergraduate Education', Change, Vol. 27, No. 6, pp.12-25.

Barr, R. B. & Tagg, J. (1995b) 'From Teaching to Learning: A New Paradigm for Undergraduate Education', Change: The magazine of higher learning, Vol. 27, No. pp.12-25.

Bean, J. C. (2011) Engaging ideas: the professor's guide to integrating writing, critical thinking, and active learning in the classroom, ed., Jossey-Bass, San Francisco.

Bergmann, J. & Sams, A. (2007) Flip Your Classroom : Reach Every Student in Every Class Every Day, ed., International Society for Tech in Ed., Eugene, UNITED STATES.

Bergtrom, G. (2011) 'Content vs. Learning: An Old Dichotomy in Science Courses', Journal of Asynchronous Learning Networks, Vol. 15, No. 1, pp.33-44.

Bloom, B. (1956) Taxonomy of Educational Objectives, Handbook I: The Cognitive Domain, ed., David McKay, Co. Inc., New York.

Bonwell, C. C. & Eison, J. A. (1991) Active Learning: Creating Excitement in the Classroom, ed., Jossey-Bass, San Francisco, CA.

Bowen, J. A. (2012) Teaching naked: How moving technology out of your college classroom will improve student learning, ed., John Wiley & Sons.

Brady, M., Seli, H. & Rosenthal, J. (2013) 'Metacognition and the Influence of Polling Systems: How Do Clickers Compare with Low Technology Systems', Educational Technology Research and Development, Vol. 61, No. 6, pp.885-902.

Bransford, J. (2000) How People Learn: Brain, Mind, Experience and School, Expanded ed., National Academies Press, Washington D.C.

Bretz, S. L., Fay, M., Bruck, L. B. & Towns, M. H. (2013) 'What Faculty Interviews Reveal about Meaningful Learning in the Undergraduate Chemistry Laboratory', Journal of Chemical Education, Vol. 90, No. 3, pp.281.

Brooks, D. C. (2016) ECAR Study of Undergraduate Students and Information Technology. 2016.

Brownstein, E. & Klein, R. (2006) 'Blogs: Applications in Science Education', Journal of College Science Teaching, Vol. 35, No. 6, pp.18-22.

Bruck, L. B., Towns, M. & Bretz, S. L. (2010) 'Faculty Perspectives of Undergraduate Chemistry Laboratory: Goals and Obstacles to Success', Journal of Chemical Education, Vol. 87, No. 12, pp.1416.

Bruff, D. (2009) Teaching with classroom response systems: Creating active learning environments, 1 ed., Jossey-Bass, San Francisco.

Carey, B. (2014) How we learn: the surprising truth about when, where, and why it happens, ed., Random House, New York.

Chambliss, D. F. & Takacs, C. G. (2014) How college works, ed., Harvard University Press, Cambridge, Massachusetts;London, England;.

Chickering, A. W. & Gamson, Z. F. (1987) 'Seven principles for good practice in undergraduate education', AAHE bulletin, Vol. 3, No. pp.7.

Chien, Y.-T., Chang, Y.-H. & Chang, C.-Y. (2016) 'Do we click in the right way? A meta-analytic review of clicker-integrated instruction', Educational Research Review, Vol. 17, No. pp.1-18.

Crouch, C. H. & Mazur, E. (2001) 'Peer Instruction: Ten years of experience and results', American Journal of Physics, Vol. 69, No. 9, pp.970-977.

Darwin, C. (1874) The descent of man: and selection in relation to sex, Rev. ed., Merrill and Baker, New York U6 - ctx_ ver=Z39.88-2004&ctx_enc=info%3Aofi%2Fenc%3AUTF-8&rfr_ id=info%3Asid%2Fsummon.serialssolutions.com&rft_val_fmt=inf o%3Aofi%2Ffmt%3Akev%3Amtx%3Abook&rft.genre=book&rft. title=The+descent+of+man&rft.au=Darwin%2C+Charles&rft. series=World+famous+books&rft.date=1874-01-01&rft. pub=Merrill+and+Baker&rft.externalDocID=a9172727&paramdi ct=en-US U7 - Book.

Davis-Berg, E. C. (2011) 'Teaching the Major Invertebrate Phyla in One Laboratory Session', American Biology Teacher, Vol. 73, No. 5, pp.281-284.

Della Sala, S. (2010) Forgetting, ed., Psychology Press, New York; Hove, East Sussex.

Duncan, D. (2005) Clickers in the Classroom: How to Enhance Science Teaching Classroom Response Systems, ed., Pearson.

Ferdig, R. & Sweetser, K. (2004) Content Delivery in the 'Blogosphere, ed.

Freeman, S., Eddy, S. L., Mcdonough, M., Smith, M. K., Okoroafor, N., Jordt, H. & Wenderoth, M. P. (2014) 'Active learning increases student performance in science, engineering, and mathematics', Proceedings of the National Academy of Sciences, Vol. 111, No. 23, pp.8410-8415.

Gladwell, M. (2008) Outliers: the story of success. New York, NY: Hachette Audio.

Hake, R. R. (1998) 'Interactive-engagement versus traditional methods: A six-thousand-student survey of mechanics test data for introductory physics courses', American Journal of Physics, Vol. 66, No. 1, pp.64-74.

Herdman, C., Diop, L. & Dickman, M. (2012) 'Carbohydrate Analysis Experiment Involving Mono-and Disaccharides with a Twist of Gly-cobiology: Two New Tests for Distinguishing Pentoses and Glycosidic Bonds', Journal of Chemical Education, Vol. 90, No. 1, pp.115-117.

Hestenes, D., Wells, M. & Swackhamer, G. (1992) 'Force concept inventory', The Physics Teacher, Vol. 30, No. 3, pp.141-158.

Hunsu, N. J., Adesope, O. & Bayly, D. J. (2016) 'A meta-analysis of the effects of audience response systems (clicker-based technologies) on cognition and affect', Computers & Education, Vol. 94, No. pp.102-119.

Kabat-Zinn, J. & Hanh, T. N. (2009) Full catastrophe living: Using the wisdom of your body and mind to face stress, pain, and illness, ed., Random House LLC.

Kornell, N. & Bjork, R. A. (2007) 'The promise and perils of self-regulated study', Psychonomic Bulletin & Review, Vol. 14, No. 2, pp.219-224.

Kruger, J. & Dunning, D. (1999) 'Unskilled and unaware of it: How difficulties in recognizing one's own incompetence lead to inflated self-assessments', Journal of Personality and Social Psychology: Attitudes and Social Cognition, Vol. 77, No. 6, pp.1121-1134.

Kuh, George D., Cruce, Ty M., Shoup, Rick, Kinzie, Jillian, Gonyea, Robert M. "Unmasking the Effects of Student Engagement on First-Year College Grades and Persistence." The Journal of Higher Education, Vol. 79, No. 5 (Sep. - Oct., 2008), pp. 540-563.

Larocco, P. (2015) Student Reaction. https://www.youtube.com/watch?v=JDJWOCm9zuM.

Laurillard, D. (2007) 'Technology, Pedagogy, and Education: Concluding Comments', Technology, Pedagogy, and Education, Vol. 16, No. 3, pp.8.

Lemke, J. L. (1990) Talking Science: Language, Learning, and Values, ed., Ablex Publishing Corporation, Norwood, NJ.

Linden, D. J. (2011) The compass of pleasure: how our brains make fatty foods, orgasm, exercise, marijuana, generosity, vodka, learning, and gambling feel so good, ed., Viking, New York.

Lortie, D. C. (2002) Schoolteacher: a sociological study, ed., University of Chicago Press, Chicago.

Magnusson, S., Krajcik, J. & Borko, H. (1999) Nature, Sources and Development of Pedagogical Content Knowledge for Science Teaching. In: GESS-NEWSOME, J. & LEDERMAN, N. G. (eds.) Examining Pedagogical Content Knowledge: The Construct and its Implications for Science Education. Kluwer Academic Publishers.

Mayer, R. E. (2009) Multimedia learning, ed., Cambridge University Press, Cambridge; New York.

Mayer, R. E., Stull, A., Deleeuw, K., Almeroth, K., Bimber, B., Chun, D., Bulger, M., Campbell, J., Knight, A. & Zhang, H. (2009) 'Clickers in college classrooms: Fostering learning with questioning methods in large lecture classes', Contemporary Educational Psychology, Vol. 34, No. 1, pp.51-57.

Mazur, E. (1997) Peer instruction: a user's manual, ed., Prentice Hall, Upper Saddle River, N.J.

McGonigal, J. (2011) Reality is broken: why games make us better and how they can change the world, ed., Penguin Press, New York.

Milner-Bolotin, M. (2012) 'Increasing interactivity and authenticity of chemistry instruction through Data Acquisition Systems and other technologies', Journal of Chemical Education, Vol. 89, No. 4, pp.477-481.

Mishra, P. & Koehler, M. J. (2006) 'Technological Pedagogical Content Knowledge: A Framework for Teacher Knowledge', Teachers College Record, Vol. 108, No. 6, pp.1017-1054.

Norman, Marie (2017) 'Extending the Shelf-Life of Your Instructional Videos', Faculty Focus, June 26, 2017.

Mysliwiec, T. H., Shibley, I., Jr. & Dunbar, M. E. (2003) 'Using Newspapers to Facilitate Learning: Learning Activities Designed to Include Current Events', Journal of College Science Teaching, Vol. 33, No. 3, pp.24

Nuland, S. B. (1994) How we die: reflections on life's final chapter, 1st ed., Alfred A. Knopf, New York.

Oliver-Hoyo, M. T. (2003) 'Designing a Written Assignment to Promote the Use of Critical Thinking Skills in an Introductory Chemistry Course', Journal of Chemical Education, Vol. 80, No. 8, pp.899-903.

Osborne, R.J., et. al. (1983) 'Learning science: A generative process,' Science Education, Vol. 67, No. 7, pp.489-508.

Perry, Hali. Excerpt from "Flipped Classroom Post-project Student Reflection," Pitt Community College, Spring 2015.

Picciano, A. G., Dziuban, C., Sloan, C., Sloan Center for Online, E. & Alfred, P. S. F. (2007) Blended learning: research perspectives, ed., The Sloan Consortium, Needham, Mass.

Popken, B. 2015. College Textbook Prices Have Rise 1,041 Percent Since 1977 [Online]. NBC News.

Rhodes, Gary. "Faculty Engagement to Enhance Student Attainment." Paper prepared for National Commission on Higher Education Attainment, 2012, http://www.acenet.edu/news-room/Documents/Faculty-Engagement-to-Enhance-Student-Attainment--Rhoades.pdf.

Richland, L. E., Kornell, N. & Kao, L. S. (2009) 'The pretesting effect: Do unsuccessful retrieval attempts enhance learning?', Journal of Experimental Psychology: Applied, Vol. 15, No. 3, pp.243.

Roach, V. A., Fraser, G. M., Kryklywy, J. H., Mitchell, D. G. & Wilson, T. D. (2016) 'The eye of the beholder: Can patterns in eye movement reveal aptitudes for spatial reasoning?', Anat Sci Educ, Vol. 9, No. 4, pp.357-66.

Roach, V. A., Fraser, G. M., Kryklywy, J. H., Mitchell, D. G. & Wilson, T. D. (2017) 'Time limits in testing: An analysis of eye movements and visual attention in spatial problem solving', Anat Sci Educ, Vol., No.

Rogers, J. W. & Cox, J. R. (2008) 'Integrating a Single Tablet PC in Chemistry, Engineering, and Physics Courses', Journal of College Science Teaching, Vol. 37, No. 3, pp.34-39.

Sadler, P. M., Woll, S., Crouse, L., Schneps, M. H., Pyramid, F. & Video (1989) A Private universe: misconceptions that block learning. Santa Monica, CA U6 - ctx_ver=Z39.88-2004&ctx_enc=info%3Aofi%2Fenc%3AUTF-8&rfr_id=info%3Asid%2Fsummon.serialssolutions.com&rft_val_fmt=info%3Aofi%2Ffmt%3Akev%3Amtx%3Ajournal&rft.genre=article&rft.atitle=A+Private+universe&rft.au=Sadler%2C+Philip+Michael&rft.au=Woll%2C+Susan&rft.au=Crouse%2C+Lindsay&rft.au=Schneps%2C+Matthew+H&rft.date=1989-01-01&rft.pub=Pyramid+Film+%26+Video&rft.externalDocID=a1714506&paramdict=en-US U7 - Video Recording: Pyramid Film & Video.

Seligin, D. (2012) 'Alternative framework, attitudes towards science and problem learning: A pilot study,' Journal of Humanities and Social Science, Vol. 2, No. 2, pp.28-41.

Senack, E. (2016) Open Textbooks: The Billion-Dollar Solution.

Shulman, Lee (1986) 'Paradigms and research programs for the study of teaching.' In M.C. Wittrock (Ed.), Handbook of research on teaching (3rd ed.). New York: Macmillan.

Shibley, I., Amaral, K. E., Shank, J. D. & Shibley, L. R. (2011) 'Designing a blended course: Using ADDIE to guide instructional design', Journal of College Science Teaching, Vol. 40, No. 6, pp.80-85.

Shibley, I., Dunbar, M. E., Mysliwiec, T. H. & Dunbar, D. A. (2008) 'Using Science Popularizations to Promote Learner-Centered Teaching: Alternatives to the Traditional Textbook', Journal of College Science Teaching, Vol. 38, No. 2, pp.54-58.

Smith, J. D. & Valentine, T. (2012) 'The Use and Perceived Effectiveness of Instructional Practices in Two-Year Technical Colleges', Journal on Excellence in College Teaching, Vol. 23, No. 1, pp.133-161.

Summers, L. H. 2012. What you (really) need to know. New York Times.

Thoreau, H. D. (1854) Walden: and on the duty of civil disobedience, ed., The Floating Press, Auckland, New Zealand.

Trilling, B., Fadel, C. & Partnership for 21st Century, S. (2009) 21st century skills: learning for life in our times, 1st ed., Jossey-Bass, San Francisco.

Umbach, Paul, and Wawrzynsky, M. 2005. "Faculty do matter: The role of college faculty in student learning and engagement." Research in Higher Education, 46,2:153-84.

U.S. Department of Education, O. O. E. T. (2017) Reimagining the Role of Technology in Higher Education: A supplement to the National Education Technology Plan. Washington, D.C.

Vines, Timothy, et. al. (2014) 'The Availability of Research Data Declines Rapidly with Article Age.' Cell Biology, Vol. 24, No. 1, pp. 94-97, January 6, 2014.

Walvoord, B. E. & Pool, K. J. (1998) 'Enhancing Pedagogical Productivity,' New Directions for Higher Education, Vol. 103, pp.35-48.

Wergin, J. F. (2001) 'Beyond carrots and sticks: What really motivates faculty', Liberal Education, Vol. 87, No. 1, pp.50.

Index

A
Abraham, J.K. 32
active learning 10, 13, 14, 32, 40, 41, 50, 53, 55, 57, 64, 92, 93, 96, 98, 101, 107, 119, 120, 125, 130, 148
active learning strategies. See active learning
Adams, P. 101
ADHD 72
Adventures in Chemistry Games 112
Allen, D. 37, 57
Ambrose, S.A. 73
American Test Anxiety Association 102
American University 143
Anatomical Sciences Education 138
Anderson 61
Angelo 67, 98
Anna Karenina 51
A Private Universe 34
assessments 38, 41, 44, 73, 75, 96, 97, 98, 99, 100, 102, 111, 126, 150
assignments 11, 16, 30, 44, 51, 52, 57, 67, 73, 74, 98, 111, 113, 116, 125, 129
axons 22

B
Balancing Chemical Equations Game 112
Barr, R.B. 43, 53
Bean, John 57
Benchling 94. See also digital notebook software
Bergmann, J. 39, 62
Bergtrom, G. 38
Biology Education 138
Bjork, R. 65
Blackboard 138. See also LMS
blended 7, 19, 54, 101, 102, 107
blended learning 11, 12, 16, 17, 18, 19, 28, 36, 37, 39, 40, 41, 96, 97, 98, 100, 136, 137, 138, 139
Blended Learning Universe 9
Blogger 85. See also blogging platforms
blogging platforms 85
blogs 85
Bloom, B. 39, 61, 68, 123, 124
Bloom's Taxonomy 39, 61, 68, 123, 124, 147
Bonwell, C.C. 57
Bowen, C.C. 88
Brady et al. 90
Bransford, J. 30

Bretz et al., 93
Brightspace. See LMS
Brooks, D.C. 17, 71, 72
Brownstein, E. 86
Bruck et al. 93
Bruff, D. 58
Bureau of Labor Statistics 74

C
Cambridge University Press v. Georgia State University 144
Campus Custom Publishing 143
Camtasia 47
Carey, B. 89
Cell Biology Education 138
Center for Academic Excellence 139
Center for Instructional Innovation 139
Center for Media and Social Impact 143
Chambliss, D.F. 109
chemical equations 112
Chemistry Games 113
Chickering, A.W. 40, 89
Chien et al. 89
classroom games 86
classroom response system. See clicker
clicker 58, 59, 62, 75, 88, 89, 90, 98, 114, 115, 120, 124, 149, 150
clicker questions 58, 59, 62, 90, 98, 114, 115, 120
cognitive load 3, 24
cognitive skills 123
coherence principle 79
collaboration 38, 64, 76, 83, 87, 131
collaborative learning 83
collaborative technologies 84
Columbia University 75
ConcepTests 120
Confucius 28
consolidation 63, 65, 67, 79
content delivery 37, 38, 53
content expert 30, 49
content knowledge 31
copyright 141, 143, 144
Copyright Clearance Center 143
course assessment 103
course content 101, 102, 103, 104, 106
course design 10, 11, 13, 18, 38, 67, 130, 131, 138
course objectives. See learning objectives
coursepacks 143
Cox, J.R. 90
critical thinking 106
Cross, D. 67, 98
Crouch, C.H. 89

Cruce, T.M. 101
Current Biology 93
cycle of learning 135

D
Darwin, C. 100
data acquisition software 94
Davis-Berg, E.C. 93
deep learning 55, 67
Della Sala, S. 63
digital notebook software 94
digital pens 91
DNA sequencers 93
Doceri 47
DoColLab 94. See also digital notebook software
DoodleCast Pro 47
dropbox 114
Dual Channel theory 26
Duncan, D. 89
Dunning, D. 99, 100, 110
Dunning-Kruger effect 99, 100, 110

E
ECAR 72, 148. See EDUCAUSE Center for Analysis and Research
Edpuzzle 74, 75, 97
educational fair use 144
EDUCAUSE 17, 72, 137
EDUCAUSE Center for Analysis and Research 72
EDUCAUSE Learning Initiative 137
Element Hangman 113
engagement 37, 38, 39, 40, 57, 89, 106, 137, 150
Engaging Ideas 127
extraneous load 25

F
F2F 14, 15, 50, 51, 53, 61, 62, 63, 64, 65, 67, 88, 89, 91, 93, 95. See face-to-face
face-to-face 36, 37, 38, 40, 41, 72, 75, 84, 87, 88, 92, 98, 124, 138, 139
Faculty Focus 73
failure 32, 63, 89
fair use 142, 143, 144, 145
Ferdig, R. 85
flipped classroom 102, 104
flipping and blending 101, 106
fluency illusion 65, 89
Force Concept Inventory 119
formative assessment 97, 98
Freeman et al. 13, 32

G
Gamson, Z.F. 40, 89
Ghost 85. See also blogging platforms
Gingras, H. 101
Gladwell, M. 136
Gonyea, R. 101
Google Docs. See software
Google Sheets 85
Google Slides 85
Google Street View 134
Google Suite 85
Gross Anatomy 132
Guidelines for Educational Fair Use 144

H
Hake, R. R. 119
Hamlet 47
Hanh, T.N. 128
Harvard College 83
Herdman et al. 93
Hestenes et al. 119
Hunsu et al. 89
hybrid learning. See blended learning

I
image principle 82
iMovies 67
imposter syndrome 30
iNACOL 9
instructional change 28
instructional design 25, 139, 153
instructor satisfaction 101
interactive videos 46
International Association for Blended Learning 137
introductory course 110
iPads 28, 47
iPhone 73
IR spectrophotometer 93

J
Jing 47
Joomla 85. See also blogging platforms
Journal of Chemical Education 138
Journal of Microbiology 138

K
Kabat-Zinn, J. 128
Kahoot 86
Kennedy, Kathryn 9

KhanAcademy 47
Kinzie, J. 101
Klein, R. 86
Kornell, N. 65
Krathwohl, D.R. 61
Kruger, J. 99, 100, 110
Kuh, G.D. 101

L
LabArchives 94. See also digital notebook software
LabFolder 94. See also digital notebook software
laboratory 58, 93, 95, 110, 131, 133, 135
laboratory learning 93
lab skills 132, 135
Lao Tzu 28
LaRocco, Phillip 75
Laurillard, Diana 77
learner-centered 53, 55, 57, 59, 67
learner-centered teaching 53, 153
learning goals 16, 44, 69, 92, 110, 114
learning management system. See LMS
Learning Management System 11, 98
learning outcomes 10, 11, 14, 15, 18, 45, 46, 81, 99, 125
lecture 102, 104
lecture capture 90
lecturing 12
Lemke, Jay 76
lesson plans 107
Linden, D.J. 60
Livescribe. See digital pen
LMS 11, 44, 50, 65, 91, 104, 111, 117, 133, 138
Locke, John 13
long-term memory 25, 27, 63, 112
Lortie, D.C. 31
LOs. See learning outcomes

M
Magna Publications 138
Magnusson et al. 31
Mahjong Chem 112
mass spectrometers 93
mastery 102
Mayer, R.E. 26, 78, 79, 81, 82, 90
Mayer et al. 90
Mazur, E. 58, 89, 90, 120, 121
McGonigal, J. 65
meta-cognition 123
microscope 93
Milner-Bolotin, M. 93
mini-lectures. See lecturers; See also lectures

modality principle 81
Muddiest Point 98. See formative assessment
multimedia 26, 27, 47, 49, 65, 78, 79, 81, 82
multimedia learning 26, 79
multimedia learning theory 26, 79
multimedia principle 81
Mysliwiec et al. 127

N
National Center for Education Statistics 71
National Educational Technology Plan 71
neural networks 24, 65
neurobiology 13, 23, 67, 136
neurons 21, 22, 24, 63
neurotransmitters 21, 22, 23, 24
New Media Consortium 137
Newton, Isaac 139
NMR spectrometers 93
non-science major 127
Norman, Marie 73
Nuland, S.B. 128

O
OER 74. See Open Educational Resource
Office of Educational Technology 71
OLC 137. See Online Learning Consortium
Oliver-Hoyo, M.T. 57
One Minute Notes 104. See also assessment
online assessment 110
Online Classroom 139
online homework 65, 66, 67
Online Learning Consortium 137
Open Educational Resource 74
OpenStax 73. See also publisher content
open textbooks 74
organelles 122
Osborne, R.J. 33
oscilloscopes 93

P
Part-Time Press 164
PCK 31, 32, 33, 34
PCR machine 93
Pedagogical Content Knowledge. See PCK
peer mentors 116
PeerWise. See summative assessment
Periodic Table Battleship 112
Periodic Table Bingo 113
Perry, H. 104
personalization principle 82

pH meters 93
Picciano et al. 36
PlayPosit. See formative assessment
POD Network 138
POGIL. See process-oriented guided inquiry learning
PollAnywhere 88
Polonius 47
Pool, K.J. 44
Popken, B. 74
Powell, Allison 9
PowerPoint 16, 26, 47, 48, 56, 78, 80, 91, 114
pre-class learning 15, 60, 122
pre-class work 15, 43, 45, 46, 48, 50, 51, 52, 62, 120, 131, 132
pre-knowledge 123, 124, 131, 135
pre-training principle 81
Prezi 91
process-oriented guided inquiry learning 62
professional development 107
Punnet squares 122

Q
Quizalize 87
quizzes 50, 116, 117

R
Rabbitt, Beth 9
redundancy principle 80
reflecting 102, 106. See also assessment
rehearse 60, 64, 65, 66, 91, 116, 127
Reimagining the Role of Technology in Higher Education 71
retention rates 106
Rhodes, G. 101
Richland et al. 66
Roach et al. 80
Rogers, J.W. 90
Rosetta Stone 47
Rspace 94. See also digital notebook software

S
Sadler, P.M. 34
sage on the stage 102
Sams, A. 39, 62
scaffold 37, 39, 41, 125
schema 16, 24, 81, 91
Scinote 94. See also digital notebook software
screencasting 47, 143
Screencast-O-Matic. See screencasting
ScreenChomp 47
ScreenFlow 47
Screenr 47

segmenting principle 81
self-testing 65, 66
Seligin, D. 32
Senack, E. 74
sensory input 27
Seven Principles for Good Practice in Undergraduate Education 39
Shibley et. al. 127
short lectures. See mini-lecturers
Shoup, R. 101
Shulman, L. 31
signaling principle 80
Smith 43
Snagit. See screen capture
Socratic Method. 10
Socrative 87
spatial contiguity principle 80
Squarespace 85. See also blogging platforms
STEM 32
stoichiometry 112
student-centered learning 71
student engagement 37, 39, 40, 57, 89, 101, 105
student evaluations 105. See also assessment
student feedback 16, 18
student responsibility 49
student retention 103
student success 12, 87, 90, 111
student surveys 104
summative assessment 98
Summers, Lawrence 83
Sweetser 85
synchronization 60

T
tabula rasa 13
Tagg 43, 53
Takacs 109
Tanner 57
Teaching and Learning Center 139
Teaching Professor 138, 139
teaching strategies 31, 34
technology 11, 16, 17, 29, 48, 52, 53, 58, 59, 60, 68, 71, 72, 73, 75, 76, 78, 85, 88, 93, 94, 95, 98, 107, 111, 125, 137, 138, 139, 148
TechSmith 47
TED 92
temporal contiguity principle 81
term paper. See writing assignments
tests 102

The Physics Teacher 138
Thoreau, H.D. 47
time on task 40, 63, 66, 113, 116, 122
transparency 68
Trilling et al. 83
Tumblr 85. See also blogging platforms
Twitter 75, 86

U
Umbach, P. 101
University of Pittsburgh 129
University of Pittsburgh Allegheny 129
University of South Dakota 48
upper-level courses 111, 113, 115, 117, 119, 121, 123, 125
U.S. Department of Education 71
UV-Vis spectrophotometers 93

V
Vala, M. 116
Valentine, T. 43
videos 46
visual aids 92
voice principle 82

W
Walvoord, B.E. 44
Wawrzynsky, M. 101
Web 2.0 28
Weebly 85. See also blogging platforms
Wergin, J.F. 140
whiteboard 47, 112
wiki 28
wiki page 68, 125
wikispaces 84
Wix 85. See also blogging platforms
WordPress.com 85. See also blogging platforms
WordPress.org 85. See also blogging platforms
working memory 25

X
XanEdu 143

Y
Yearwood, Dave 48
YouTube 47, 58, 76, 92

FAQ's...

How to place an order:
Orders may be placed **by mail** to Part-Time Press, P.O. Box 130117, Ann Arbor, MI 48113-0117, **by phone/fax** at (734)930-6854, and **online** at https://www.Part-TimePress.com.

How much do I pay if I order multiple copies?
Part-Time Press books have quantity discounts available:

10-49 copies—10% discount

50-99 copies— 20% discount

100 or more copies—30% discount

How may I pay for orders?
Orders may be placed with **a purchase order** or may be paid by **check**, **PayPal** or **credit card** (Visa/Mastercard, Discover or AMEX.)

How will my order be shipped?
Standard shipping to a continental U.S. street address is via **UPS-Ground Service**. Foreign shipments or U.S. post office box addresses go through the **U.S. Postal Service** and express shipments via **UPS-2nd Day**, or **UPS-Next Day**. Shipping and handling charges are based on the dollar amount of the shipment, and a fee schedule is shown on the next page.

What if I'm a reseller like a bookstore or wholesaler?
Resellers get a standard **20% discount** off of the single copy retail price, or may choose to receive the multiple copy discount.

Part-Time Press Books: Order Form

Qty	Title	Unit $$	Total
	The Power of Blended Learning in the Sciences	$20.00	
	Blended Learning and Flipped Classrooms, 1st ed.	$20.00	
	Teaching in the Sciences	$20.00	
	Handbook for Adjunct/Part-Time Faculty, 7th ed.	$20.00	
	Handbook II: Advanced Teaching Strategies	$20.00	
	Teaching Strategies and Techniques, 6th ed.	$15.00	
	Going the Distance: A Handbook for Part-Time & Adjunct Faculty Who Teach Online, Rev. 1st ed.	$15.00	
	Getting Down to Business	$20.00	
		Subtotal	
		Shipping	
		Total	

Shipping Schedule:
1-4 books   *$6.00*
5+ books   *8 percent of the purchase price*

Part-Time Press: P.O. Box 130117, Ann Arbor, MI 48113-0117
Fax/Phone: 734-930-6854 Email: orders@part-timepress.com
Order securely online: https://www.Part-TimePress.com
Canadian customers order securely online: http://ca.part-timepress.com

Purchaser/Payment Information

☐ Check (payable to The Part-Time Press)
☐ Credit Card # _____ Exp._____
   CVV# _____
☐ Purchase Order # _____
Name _____
Institution _____
Address _____ City/ST/Zip _____
Ph:_____ Email: _____